MW01130927

Sarah Re

ENGLISH: FAST TRACK LEARNING FOR FRENCH SPEAKERS.

The 1000 most used English words with 3.000 phrase examples for French speaking people.

Focus your English learning on the most frequently used words
Learn just the 1000 words you need for everyday life.

Published by UNITEXTO

UNITEXTO
Digital Publishing

TABLE OF CONTENTS

The most used words

RANKING: 001–100

The most used words

1. The Le/La	2. Of De/Du	3. And Et	4. To A/Au	5. A Un/Une
6. In Dans	7. Is Est	8. You Tu	9. Are Sommes/Etes Sont	10. For Pour
11. That Que/Ça	12. Or Ou	13. It Le/La/Il	14. As Comme/Alors	15. Be Etre/Soit
16. On Sur	17. Your Ton	18. With Avec	19. Can Peux/Peut	20. Have Ai/Avons/Dois
21. This Ce/Cette Ça	22. An Un/Une	23. By Par	24. Not Pas	25. But Mais
26. At A/Au/En	27. From De/Du	28. I Je/Moi	29. They Ils/Elles	30. More Plus
31. Will -Ra/-Ront	32. If Si	33. Some Un peu Certain	34. There Là/Là-bas	35. What Que/Qu'/ Quoi
36. About A Propos/ Concernant	37. Which Quel/Quelle	38. When Quand	39. One Un/Une/Celui	40. Their Leur/Leurs
41.	42.	43.	44.	45.

All Tout/Tous	Also Aussi	How Comment	Many Beaucoup	Do Faire
46. Has A	47. Most Majorité Plus	48. People Gens	49. Other Autre	50. Time Temps
51. So Beaucoup/ Très	52. Was Étais/Était	53. We Nous	54. These Ces-Ceux	55. May Peux/Peut
56. Like Aime	57. Use Utiliser	58. Into En	59. Than Que	60. Up Haut
61. Out Dehors	62. Who Qui	63. Them Eux/Les	64. Make Faire	65. Because Parceque/ À Cause
66. Such Tel/Telle	67. Through À Travers	68. Get Obtenir/ Tenir	69. Work Travailler	70. Even Pair/ Même
71. Different Différent	72. Its Son/Sa/Ses	73. No Non	74. Our Notre Nos	75. New Neuf/Nouveau Nouvelle
76. Film Film	77. Just Juste Seulement	78. Only Seul Seulement	79. See Voir	80. Used Utilisé Habitué
81. Good Bon/Bien	82. Water Eau	83. Been Été	84. Need A Besoin	85. Should Devrait
86. Very	87. Any	88. History	89. Often	90. Way

Très	N'importe Quel	Histoire	Souvent	Manière Route
91. Well Bien	92. Art Art	93. Know Connaitre Savoir	94. Were Étais Etaient	95. Then Ensuite
96. My Mon	97. First Premier	98. Would Pourrions	99. Money Argent	100. Each Chaque

1. *the/le-la*

The sky is clear.	*Le* ciel est clair
The boy plays with the ball.	*Le* garçon jour avec le balon
The girl looks pretty in the pink dress.	*La* fille est jolie dans sa tenue rose

2. *of/de*

The dog *of* my son is black	Le chien *de* mon fils est noir
I am short *of* money.	Je suis à court *d'*argent
I am proud *of* my son.	Je suis fier *de* mon fils

3. *and/et*

Jack can read *and* write.	Jack peut lire *et* écrire
Please stand here *and* wait.	S'il vous plait restez ici *et* attendez
Jill likes bread *and* butter.	Jill aime le pain *et* le beurre

4. *to/à-au*

I went *to* the city	Je suis allé *à* la ville
I went *to* the store to buy a pen.	Je sui sallé *au* magazin pour acheter un stylo
He will come to our home tomorrow.	Il viendra *à* notre maison demain

5. *a/un-une*

A committee has been set up.	*Un* comité a été organisé
The place is *a* bit far from here.	L'endroit est *un* peu loin d'ici
A cat is crossing the street.	*Un* chat traverse la route

6. *in/dans*

There is water *in* the glass.	Il y a de l'eau *dans* le verre
The girl *in* bar looks good.	La fille *dans* le bar semble jolie
What is *in* the blue box?	Qu'est ce qu'il y a *dans* la boite bleu?

7. *is/est*

What *is* your name?	Quell *est* ton nom ?
The man *is* definitely deaf.	L'homme *est* complétement sourd
He *is* here for a purpose.	Il *est* ici pour une raison

8. *you/tu*

What have *you* done?	Qu'est ce que *tu* as fais ?
You will not come early.	*Tu* ne viendras pas plus tôt
You should improve your handwriting.	*Tu* dois améliorer ton écriture

9. *are/sommes-êtes-sont*

All of them *are* not poor.	Ils ne *sont* pas tous pauvres
We *are* here now.	Nous *sommes* ici maitenant
When *are* you coming back?	Quand *êtes*-vous de retour

10. *for/pour*

Do not be late *for* work.	Ne sois pas en retard *pour* le travail
I studied *for* the exam.	J'ai étudié *pour* l'examen
It is time *for* us to leave the house.	Il est temps *pour* nous de quitter la maison

11. *that/que-ça*

I hope *that* he will succeed.	J'espère *qu'*il réussira
I should not have said *that.*	Je n'aurai pas du dire *ça*
I thought *that* James was very kind.	Je pensais *que* James était très gentil.

12. *or/ou*

It is now *or* never.	C'est maintenant *ou* jamais

I will go, rain *or* shine.	Je partirai, qu'il ait de la pluie *ou* du soleil
Did you come by bus *or* train?	êtes-vous venu par train *ou* pas bus?

13. *it/le-la-il*

Do not touch *it.*	Ne *le* touche pas
Give *it* to him.	Donne *le* lui
I will see to *it.*	Je *le* vérifierai

14. *as/comme-alors*

Tom acted *as* my guide.	Tom agit *comme* mon guide
We spoke *as* we walked	Nous parlons *comme* nous marchons
It was just *as* I thought	C'était *comme* j'ai pensé

15. *be/être-soit*

Do not *be* sad	Ne *sois* pas triste
He must *be* tired	Il doit *être* fatigué
She must *be* sick	Elle doit *être* malade

16. *on/sur*

Your shirt is on the window.	Ta chemise est *sur* la fenêtre

Please put the pen *on* the chair	Mettez s'il vous plait le stylo *sur* la chaise
Put the book *on* the table	Posez le libre *sur* la table

17. *your/ton-ta-tes*

I want to see *your* mother	Je veux voir *ta* mère
I appreciate *your* concern	J'apprécie *ton* inquiétude
Be kind to *your* parents	Sois gentil avec *tes* parents

18. *with/avec*

What should I do *with* it?	Que dois-je faire *avec*?
Bring the credi card *with* you.	Apporte la carte de crédit *avec* toi
Mix the solution *with* sugar.	Mélange la solution *avec* du sucre

19. *can/peux-peut*

Jill *can* jump high	Jill *peut* sauter haut
I *can* play tennis	Je *peux* jouer le tennis
He *can* be relied on	On *peut* compter sur lui

20. *have/ai-avons-dois*

I *have* three dogs.	J'*ai* trois chiens
I *have* to go home.	Je *dois* aller à la maison

We *have* dinner.	*Nous avons le diner*

21. *this/ce-cet-cette-ça*

This makes no sense.	*Ça* n'a aucun sens
This bird cannot fly.	*Cet* oiseau ne peut pas voler
This is a small book.	*Ce* livre est petit

22. *an/un-une*

He is *an* author	C'est *un* autheur
I have *an* idea	J'ai *une* idée
He slept *an* hour	Il a dormi *une* heure

23. *by/par*

John came *by* bus.	John est venu *par* bus
I will come *by* plane tomorrow	Je viendrai *par* avion demain
Let us go *by* car.	Allons *par* voiture

24. *not/pas*

Jill is *not* tall.	Jill n'est *pas* grand
Jack may *not* come.	Jack peut ne *pas* venir
Derek is *not* a teacher.	Derek n'est *pas* un enseignant

25. *but/mais*

Romeo tried hard, *but* failed.	Romeo a durement essayé, *mais* a échoué
Excuse me, *but* I am not feeling well.	Excuse-moi, *mais* je ne me sens pas très bien
I am a teacher *but* he is not.	Je un enseigant, *mais* il ne l'est pas.

26. *at/à-au-en*

I will go at the time of inscription	j'irai *au* moment de l'inscription
Did you speak *at* all?	Parlez vous *du* tout?
You must go *at* any moment	Vous devez partir *à* tout moment

27. *from/de-du*

David came *from* London yesterday.	David est venu *de* Londres hier
Where do you come *from?*	*D'*où viens-tu?
The man *from* the bar looked suspicious.	L'homme *du* bar parraissait suspicieux

28. *I/je-moi*

I am a very honest man.	*Je* suis un homme très honnête
I do not like her at all.	*Je* ne l'aime pas du tout
Where do *I* sign?	Où dois-*je* signer?

29. *they/ils-elles*

They admire each other.	*Ils* s'admirent mutuellement
They can speak French.	*Elles* peuvent parler français
They are playing chess.	*Ils* jouent aux echecs

30. *more/plus*

Jennifer has *more* books than you.	Jennifer a *plus* de libres que toi
I will not see her any *more.*	Je la verrai *plus*
Could you drive *more* slowly?	Peux-tu conduire *plus* doucement

31. *will/-rai--rons*

A thousand dollars *will* do.	Mille dollars fe*ront*
I *will* gladly help you.	Je t'aide*rai* avec joie
They *will* be very glad.	Ils se*ront* très contents

32. *if/si-s'*

I will come *if* necessary.	Je viendrai *si* nécessaire
I do not mind *if* it is cold.	Ça ne me dérange pas *s'*il fait froid
Jack will come even *if* he is angry.	Jack viendra même *s'*il est furieux

33. *Some/un peu-certain*

I wish to visit Singapore *some* day.	Je souhaite visiter Singapoure un

	certain jour
I guess Mary will need *some* help there.	Je pense que Mary aura besoin d'un *peu* d'aide
I put *some* cream in the coffee.	J'ai mis un *peu* de crême dans le café

34. *There/là- là-bas*

My teachers made me go *there.*	Mes professeurs m'ont fait partir *là-bas*
I saw Luke standing *there.*	J'ai vu Luke debout *là*
You can go *there* on a boat.	Tu peux aller *là-bas* en bateau

35. *What/que-qu'-quoi*

What have I done to deserve this?	*Qu'*ai-je fais pour mériter ça?
What is your name?	C'est *quoi* ton nom?
What is the matter?	C'est *quoi* le problème?

36. *About/à propos-concernant*

What is the commotion all *about?*	Cette agittion est *à propos* de quoi?
She complained *about* the noise.	Elle s'est plainte *concernant* le bruit
Be careful *about* what you eat.	Sois méfiant *à propos* de ce que tu manges

37. *Which/quell-quelle*

Which subject do you like best?	*Quel* sujet aimes-tu le plus?
Which of these balls is yours?	*Quelle* balles de celles-là est la tienne?
Which book did you refer to?	A *quel* libre te réfères-tu?

38. *When/quand*

When was the work finished?	*Quand* est ce que le travail était fini?
When will you leave?	*Quand* partiras-tu?
When did you get home?	*Quand* est-tu rentré à la maison?

39. *One/un-une-celui*

This *one* is more beautiful.	*Celui* là est plus beau
I studied for *one* hour.	J'ai étudié pendant *une* heure
Choose the *one* you like.	Choisis *un* qui te plait

40. *Their/leur-leurs*

Children should listen to *their* parents.	Les enfants doivent écouter *leurs* parents
Do not talk about them behind *their* backs.	Ne parle pas d'eux derrière *leurs* dos
They are on bad terms with *their* neighbors.	Il sont en mauvais termes avec *leurs* voisins

41. *All/tout-tous*

Jim looked *all* around.	Jim a regardé *tout* autour
He kept talking *all* day.	Il a parlé *toute* la journée
She did not study at *all.*	Elle n'a pas étudié du *tout*

42. *Also/aussi*

The girl was *also* there.	La fille était *aussi* ici
I can *also* speak French.	Je peux *aussi* parler français
The boy can *also* play hockey.	Le garçon peut *aussi* jouer au hockey

43. *How/comment*

How will you do this?	*Comment* feras-tu ça?
How I am I supposed to know this fact?	*Comment* suis-je sensé connaitre ce fait?
How are you?	*Comment* vas-tu?

44. *Many/beaucoup-combien*

Not *many* people know of this.	Pas *beaucoup* de gens sont au courant
I have *many* books in my shelf.	J'ai *beaucoup* de libre sur mon étagère
How *many* chocolates do you have?	*Combien* as-tu de chocolat ?

45. *Do/fais*

Do as you like.	*Fais* comme bon te semble

Never *do* this again.	Ne *fais* plus jamais ça de nouveau
Always *do* things differently.	*Fais* toujours les choses différemment

46. *Has/a*

There *has* been an accident.	Il y *a* eu un accident
Nancy *has* dry hair.	Nancy *a* des cheuveux secs
She *has* her own room.	Elle *a* sa propre chambre

47. *Most/ la majorité-plus*

Most people think positive.	La *majorité* des gens pensent positivement
I was in Bangkok *most* of the winter.	J'étais à Bangkok la *majorité* de l'hiver
What is his *most* recent novel?	Quel est le romand le *plus* récent?

48. *People/gens*

Not many *people* think like that.	Pas beaucoup de *gens* pensent comme ça
Be kind to old *people.*	Sois gentil avec les *gens* vieux
They are good *people.*	Ils sont des *gens* bien

49. Other/autre

We all love each *other.*	Nous nous aimons les uns les *autres*
I met her the *other* day.	Je l'ai rencontré *l'autre* jour

They smiled at each *other.*	Ils ont souri l'un à *l'autre*

50. *Time/temps*

It is about *time.*	C'est à propos du *temps*
Have a good *time.*	Passe du beau *temps*
I need more *time.*	J'ai besoin de plus de *temps*

51. *So/beaucoup-très*

Martha looks *so* tired.	Martha parait *très* fatiguée
He won't endure *so* long.	Il ne supportera pas *très* longtemps
She hated him *so* much.	Elle le déteste *beaucoup*

52. *Was/étais-était*

Jim *was* in Japan.	Jim *était* au Japon
She *was* very happy.	Ella *était* très heureuse
I *was* out all day.	J'*étais* dehors toute la journée

53. *We/nous*

We are not amused.	*Nous* ne sommes pas amusés
We go there often.	*Nous* allons souvent là-bas
We must keep calm.	*Nous* devons rester calmes

54. *These/ces-ceux*

These dogs are big.	*Ces* chiens sont grands
These scissors cut well.	*Ces* ciseaux coupent bien
Can you mail *these* for me?	Peux-tu poster *ceux*-là

55. *May/peux-peut*

May I ask you a question?	Est ce que je *peux* te poser une question?
It *may* rain tomorrow.	Il *peut* pleuvoir demain
You *may* go.	Tu *peux* partir

56. *Like/aime*

I do not *like* her at all.	Je ne *l'aime* pas du tout
She may not *like* these.	Elle peut ne pas *aimer* ceux-là
Would you *like* to hear a song?	*Aimes*-tu écouter une chanson?

57. *Use/utiliser*

Can I *use* a credit card?	Est ce que je peux *utiliser* une carte de crédit
We *use* a lot of water every day.	Nous *utilisons* beaucoup d'eau quotidienement
It is of no *use* asking him again.	Lui demander ne será d'aucune *utilité*

58. *Into/en-au*

Get *into* the car.	Monte *en* voiture
He ran *into* debt.	Il est passé *en* endettement
Tim got *into* bed.	Tim est parti *au* lit

59. *Than/que*

Jim is definitely better *than* me.	Jim est carrément meilleur *que* moi
I am shorter *than* you.	Je suis plus petit *que* toi
She swims better *than* I do.	Elle nage mieux *que* moi

60. *Up/allumer-haut*

Turn *up* the TV.	*Allume* la télé
I called him *up*.	Je l'ai appelé *haut*
Prices of electronics went *up*.	Les prix de l'électronique sont montés très *haut*

61. *Out/dehors-éteindre*

I heard him go *out*.	Je l'ai entendu aller *dehors*
She threw him *out*.	Elle l'a jeté *dehors*
Put *out* the light, please.	*Éteins* la lumière s'il te plait

62. *Who/qui*

Who do you think I am?	*Qui* penses-tu que je suis?
Go and see *who* it is.	Va voir *qui* est-ce
Who broke the vase?	*Qui* a cassé le vase?

63. *Them/eux-les*

I do not know *them.*	Je ne *les* connais pas
We sometimes see *them*	Nous *les* voyons parfois
I do not like any of *them.*	Je n'aime aucun d'entre *eux*

64. *Make/fais-fait*

We all *make* mistakes.	On *fait* tous des erreurs
How did you *make* it?	Comment tu l'as *fais*?
What did Martha *make*?	Qu'a *fait* Martha?

65. *Because/parceque-à cause*

She cannot come *because* she is sick,.	Elle ne peut pas venir *parcequ'elle* est malade
I am hungry *because* I skipped lunch.	J'ai faim *parceque* j'ai sauté le déjeuner
We lost our electricity *because* of the storm.	Nous avons plus d'électricité *à cause* de la témpête

66. *Such/tel-telle*

I have never heard of *such* a thing	Je n'ai jamais entendu une *telle* chose

He cannot have done *such* a thing.	I l n'aurrait pas pu faire une *telle* chose
You should not say *such* things to her.	Tu ne dois pas lui dire de *telles* choses

67. *Through/à travers*

The arrow went *through* the apple.	La flèche es tallé *à travers* la pomme
He was looking *through* me.	Il regardait *à travers* moi
The hot knife sliced *through* the butter.	Le couteau chaud a glissé *à travers* le beurre

68. *Get/obtenir*

Can you *get* me a chocolate?	Peux-tu *m'obtenir* un chocolat?
What can I *get* for you?	Que puis-je *t'obtenir*?
Where did you *get* those?	Où as-tu *obtenu* ceux-là?

69. *Work/travail*

Please get back to your *work*.	S'il te plait retourne à ton *travail*
Complete your pending *work* first.	Termine d'abord ton *travail* en suspens
Can you do this *work* for me?	Peux-tu faire ce *travail* pour moi?

70. *Even/pair-même*

Ten is an *even* number.	Dix est un nombre *pair*
She did not *even* try to help.	Elle n'a *même* pas essayé d'aider

I have to go *even* if it rains.	Je dois aller *même* s'il pleut

71. *Different/different*

The shirt looks really *different.*	Cette chemise est *différente*
My phone is *different* from yours.	Mon téléphone est *différent* du tien
Did you go to *different* colleges?	Es-tu parti à *différents* collèges?

72. *Its/ sa-ce-ses*

Please put it back in *its* place.	S'il te plait remes-le à *sa* place
It is not mine.	*Ce* n'est pas le mien
The company fired all *its* employees.	La companie a licencié tous *ses* employés

73. *No/non-personne-pas*

No one can tell.	*Personne* ne peut dire
I have *no* money.	Je n'ai *pas* d'érgent
No, thank you.	*Non,* merci

74. *Our/notre-nos*

We will do *our* best.	Nous ferons de *notre* mieux
Welcome to *our* home.	Bienvenue dans *notre* maison
We see with *our* eyes.	Nous voyons avec *nos* yeux

75. *New/neuf-nouveau-nouvelle*

The book is almost *new.*	Le libre est presque *neuf*
I bought a *new* phone for her.	J'ai acheté un *nouveau* téléphone
She needs a *new* pair of shoes.	Elle a besoin d'un *nouvelle* paire de chaussure

76. *Film/film*

What kind of a *film* is ?	Quel type de *film* est-ce?
The *film* was really engrossing.	Le *film* était vraiment palpitant
Did you watch the *film?*	As-tu vu le *film*?

77. *just/juste-seulement*

I am *just* watching TV.	Je regarde *juste* la télé
He has *just* arrived.	Il vient *juste* d'arriver
I am *just* looking.	Je regarde *seulement*

78. *only/seul seulement*

This is the *only* book I have.	C'est le *seul* libre que j'ai
I *only* spent a couple of dollars.	J'ai dépensé *seulement* deux dollars
I *only* slept 3 hours.	J'ai dormi 3 heures *seulement*

79. *see/voir-vu*

Please come and *see* this spectacle.	S'il te plait viens *voir* ce spectacle
Did you *see* that?	As-tu *vu* celà?
I could *see* him from a distance.	Je peux le *voir* de loin

80. *used/utilisé-s'habituer*

He has never *used* such a car	Il n'a jamais *utilisé* une telle voiture
I need to get *used* to this climate	Je dois m'*habituer* à ce climat
I have never *used* his shaving kit.	Je n'ai jamais *utilisé* son kit de rasage

81. *good/bon-bien*

I was never *good* in Physics.	Je n'ai jamais été *bon* en physique
Jill scored *good* marks in history.	Jill a de *bonnes* notes en histoires
The behavior of Jim was *good*	Le comportement de Jim était *bon*

82. *water/eau*

The dog needs some *water*	Le chien a besoin d'un peu *d'eau*
Water is the elixir of life	*L'eau* est l'élixir de la vie
Can I have a glass of *water?*	Puis-je avoir un verre *d'eau*?

83. *been/été*

I have never *been* to London.	Je n'ai jamais *été* à Londres
Have you *been* to the market?	Tu as *été* au marché?

I have *been* there twice.	J'ai *été* là-bas deux fois

84. *need/besoin*

I *need* help.	J'ai *besoin* d'aide
I *need* a favor.	J'ai *besoin* d'une faveur
I *need* help.	J'ai *besoin* d'aide

85. *should/devrais*

How *should* I know?	Comment *devrais*-je savoir?
He *should* sleep.	Il *devrait* dormir
You *should* go.	Il *devrait* partir

86. *very* (adverb)/beaucoup-très

I love her *very* much.	Je l'aime *beaucoup*
The pizza is *very* hot.	La pizza est *très* chaude
The juice is *very* cold.	Le jus est *très* froid

87. *any/quelque-aucune*

Do you have *any* information?	As-tu *quelque* information?
I don't have *any* fresh clothes.	Je n'ai *aucun* vêtement frais
Do you have *any* change?	As-tu *quelque* monnaie?

88. *history/histoire*

She has lost her *history* books.	Elle a perdu ses livres *d'histoire*
History is my favorite subject.	*L'histoire* est mon sujet préféré
Do you know the *history* of this place?	Connais-tu *l'histoire* de cet endroit?

89. *often/ souvent-fréquence*

I *often* travel.	Je voyage *souvent*
How *often* do you visit him?	À quelle *fréquence* le visitez-vous
I go there *often.*	Je vais là-bas *souvent*

90. *way/chemin*

Which *way* is the salon?	Quel est le *chemin* du salon?
Do you know the *way* to the shop?	Connais-tu le *chemin* de la boutique?
I have lost my *way.*	J'ai perdu mon *chemin*?

91.*well/bien*

She sings *well.*	Elle chante *bien*
Do you know him very well ?	Vous le connaissez très *bien*?
I am not feeling *well* now.	Je ne me sens pas *bien*

92. *art/art*

I am not really an *art* lover.	Je ne sui spas vraiment un amoureux

	de *l'art*
The works of *art* deserves special praise.	Les travaux *d'art* méritent un éloge spécial
The museum displayed lovely pieces of *art.*	Le musée expose de très belles pièces *d'art*

93. *know/savoir/connaitre*

You should *know* it.	Tu devrais le *savoir*
I do not think I *know* her well.	Je ne pensé pas que je la *connais* bien
Do you *know* him?	Tu le *connais*?

94. *were/être-étions-étiez*

I wish I *were* rich.	Je souhaite *être* riche
We *were* all tired.	Nous *étions* tous fatigués
What *were* you doing?	Qu'*étiez*-vous en train de faire?

95. *then/ensuite-donc*

I was eating lunch *then.*	J'étais en train de déjeuner *ensuite*
What did you do *then?*	Qu'as-tu fais *ensuite*?
We were younger *then.*	Tu étais plus jeune *donc*

96. *my/mon*

I cannot find *my* pen.	Je netrouve pas *mon* stylo

Do you have *my* number?	As-tu *mon* numéro?
My brother is very close to me.	*Mon* frère est très proche de moi

97. *first/premier*

I was the *first* to get reprimanded.	J'étais le *premier* à se faire reprimendé
Give me the *first* book on the shelf.	Donne moi le *premier* libre sur l'étagère
He came *first* in the class.	Il est venu *premier* en classe

98.*would/-rait_ -rais*

She *would* like to be professional pianist.	Elle aime*rait* être une pianiste professionnelle
I *would* love to visit New York.	Je souhaite*rais* visiter New York
I *would* never do this.	Je ne fe*rais* jamais ça

99. *money/argent*

Do you have enough *money* in the bag?	As-tu assez *d'argent* dans le sac?
Please give me back my *money.*	S'il vous plait, rendez moi mon *argent*
Where is the *money?*	Où est *l'argent*?

100. *each/chacun-chaque*

We love each one	Nous aimons *chacun*
There is one chocolate for *each* person	Il y a un chocolat pour *chaque*

	personne
Each person has responsabilities	*Chaque* personne a des responsabilités

RANKING: 101–200
The most used words

101. Over Fini	102. World Monde	103. Information Information	104. Map Carte	105. Find Trouver
106. Where Où	107. Much Plus	108. Take Prendre	109. Two Deux	110. Want Veux
111. Important Important	112. Family Famille	113. Those Ce/Ces	114. Example Exemple	115. While Pendant
116. He Il	117. Look Regarder	118. Government Gouvernement	119. Before Avant	120. Help Aider
121. Between Entre	122. Go Aller	123. Own Propre	124. However Cependant	125. Business Afffaires
126. Us Nous	127. Great Grand/ Magnifique	128. His Ses-Son	129. Being Etre	130. Another Autre
131. Health Santé	132. Same Pareil/Même	133. Study Etudie	134. Why Pourquoi	135. Few Quelque
136. Game Jeu	137. Might Pourrais	138. Think Pense Réfléchis	139. Free Gratuit	140. Too Aussi/Trop
141. Had Eu	142. Hi Salut	143. Right Raison/Droite	144. Still Toujours	145. System Système
146.	147.	148.	149.	150.

After Après	Computer Ordinateu	Best Mejor	Must Debe	Her Ella
151. Life Vie	152. Since Depuis	153. Could/ Pourrions- Pourrait	154. Does Est	155. Now Maintenant
156. During Durant	157. Learn Apprendre	158. Around Autour	159. Usually D'habitude	160. Form Forme
161. Meat Viande	162. Air Jour	163. Day Jour	164. Place Lieu	165. Become Deviennent Devenu- Devenir
166. Number Numéro	167. Public Publique- Public	168. Read Lis	169. Keep Garder	170. Part Partie
171. Start Démarre	172. Year Année	173. Every Chaque	174. Field Champ	175. Large Grande
176. Once Une Fois	177. Available Disponible	178. Down Tombée	179. Give Abandonne Donne	180. Fish Poissons
181. Human Humain	182. Both Deux	183. Local Local	184. Sure Certainement- Certain	185. Something Quelque chose
186. Without Sans	187. Come Viendrai- Venir	188. Me Me-M'	189. Back Retour Rentré	190. Better Mieux
191.	192.	193.	194.	195.

General Général	Process Processus	She Elle	Heat Réchauffe Chaleur	Thanks Merci
196. Specific Spécifique	197. Enough Assez	198. Long Long-Longue	199. Lot Beaucoup	200. Hand Main

101. *over/fini-par*

It is all *over.*	Tout est *fini*
What is *over* there?	Qu'y a-t-il *par* là ?
It is all *over* for us.	C'est *fini* pour nous

102. *world/monde*

Derek has traveled all over the *world.*	Derek a voyagé dans le *monde* entier
What in the *world* are you doing?	Que fais-tu dans le *monde* ?
The *world* does not revolve around you.	Le *monde* ne tourne pas autour de toi

103. *information/information*

The *information* that you gave is incorrect.	L'*information* que tu as donnée est incorrecte
Do you have *information* about your father?	As-tu une *information* à propos de ton père ?
The *information* in the booklet is enough.	L'*information* dans le livret est suffisante

104. *map/carte*

This is a road *map.*	C'est une *carte* de la route
Can you draw a *map* for me?	Peux-tu dessiner une *carte* pour moi ?
Take a look at this *map.*	Regarde cette *carte*

105. *find/trouver*

Can you *find* it?	Peux-tu le *trouver* ?
I have to *find* it.	Je dois le *trouver*
Susan cannot *find* a job.	Susan ne peut pas *trouver* un travail

106. *where/où*

Where are you?	*Où es-tu ?*
Where is this building?	*Où est le batiment ?*
Where is my book?	*Où est mon livre ?*

107. *much/plus*

There is nothing *much* you can do.	Il n'y a rien de *plus* que tu puisses faire
I have nothing *much* to say.	Je n'ai *plus* rien à dire
There has not been *much* progress	Il n'y a pas eu *plus* de progrès

108. *take/prendre-prend*

Do not forget to *take* your phone.	N'oublie pas de *prendre* ton téléphone

Take the pens with you.	*Prends les stylos avec toi*
Take Jill along with you.	*Prend Jill avec toi*

109. *two/deux*

I have *two* editions of the same book.	J'ai *deux* éditions du même livre
Give me *two* pence, please.	Donne moi *deux* pences s'il te plait
Give me *two* packs of these.	Donne moi *deux* paquets de ceux-là

110. *want/veux*

I *want* a refund immediately.	Je *veux* un remboursement immédiatement
I *want* a musical instrument.	Je *veux* un instrument musical
What do you *want?*	Qu'est ce que tu *veux* ?

111. *important/important-importante*

Is this document really *important?*	Est-ce que ce document est vraiment *important* ?
I have an *important* meeting tomorrow.	J'ai une réunion *importante* demain
It is very *important* to follow a strict diet.	C'est très *important* de suivre un régime strict

112. *family/famille*

My *family* is important to me.	Ma *famille* est importante pour moi
He has left his *family.*	Il a quitté sa *famille*
Her *family* is very large.	Sa *famille* est très large

113. *those/ce-ces*

Those are my books.	*Ce* sont mes livres
Those oranges are very big.	*Ces* organges sont très grandes
She looks very odd in *those* clothes.	Elle semble très bizarre dans *ces* vêtements

114. *example/exemple*

This painting is an *example* of his work.	Cette peinture est un *exemple* de son travail
Here you can find an *example*	Ici vous pouvez trouver un *exemple*
He is *example* to his younger brothers.	Il est un *exemple* pour ses petits frères

115. *while/pendant*

I washed the dishes *while* you were away.	J'ai lavé les assiettes *pendant* que tu étais dehors
Complete the work *while* I cook.	Termine le travail *pendant* que je cuisine
I will have lunch *while* you come here.	Je déjeunerai *pendant* que tu arrives ici

116. *he/il*

He is a man of great character.	*Il* est un homme de grand caractère
I do not think *he* deserved this.	Je ne pense pas qu'*il* mérite ça
He should be here by now.	*Il* devrait être ici maintenant

117. *look/regrade*

Look at her face.	*Regrade* son visage
The *look* on his face tells all.	Le *regard* dans son visage dit tout
I need to *look* through all these.	Je dois *regarder* ceux-là

118. *government/gouvernement*

The *government* is doing nothing	Le *gouvernement* ne fait rien
We have no control over the *government*	Nous n'avons aucun contrôle sur le *gouvernement*
A stable *government* requires a democracy.	Un *gouvernement* stable nécessite une démocratie

119. *before/avant*

Come home *before* nine.	Rentre à la maison *avant* neuf heures
He reads *before* bedtime.	Il lit *avant* de dormir
I have not met her *before.*	Je ne l'ai pas rencontré *avant*

120. *help/aide-aider*

She asked for *help* in the middle of the	Elle a demandé de l'*aide* au mileu de la

night.	nuit
The police is there to *help* you.	La police est ici pour *aider*
I was able to *help* him.	Je pouvais l'*aider*

121. *between/entre*

One must read *between* the lines.	Un doit lire *entre* les lignes
I was sitting *between* Jack and Tom.	J'étais assis *entre* Jack et Tom
The doctor advised to eat *between* meals.	Le médecin a conseillé de manger *entre* les repas

122. *go/aller-va*

Where did you *go?*	Où es-tu *allé* ?
Please *go* to your room.	S'il te plait *va* à ta chambre
I have nowhere to *go.*	Je n'ai nulle part où *aller*

123. *own/propre*

Jim has his *own* room.	Jim a sa *propre* chambre
I have a house of my *own.*	J'ai ma *propre* maison
He is afraid of his *own* shadow.	Il a peur de son *propre* ombre

124. *however/cependant*

Tim has money *however* he is not happy.	Tim a l'argent, *cependant* il n'est pas heureux

However, he was afraid of dogs.	*Cependant*, il avait peur des chiens
However, I want to come tomorrow	*Cependant*, je veux venir demain

125. *business/affaires*

His *business* is doing rather well.	Ses *affaires* vont très bien
This is none of your *business.*	Ce n'est pas de tes *affaires*
What is the nature of your *business?*	Quelle est la nature de tes *affaires* ?

126. *us/nous*

Come with *us.*	Viens avec *nous*
Come and help *us.*	Viens et aide-*nous*
Stay here with *us.*	Reste ici avec *nous*

127. *great/grand-magnifique*

Roosevelt was a *great* leader.	Roosvelt était un *grand* leader
He is a *great* statesman.	Il est un *grand* homme d'Etat
Monaco is a *great* place for the retirees.	Monaco est un lieu *magnifique* pour les retraités

128. *his/ses-son*

Where are *his* books?	Où sont *ses* livres ?
His wallet is missing from the drawer.	*Son* portefeuille est manquant du tirroir

I *might* go there with her.	Je *pourrais* allez là-bas avec elle
He *might* not be happy.	Il pourrait ne pas être *heureux*
A knife *might* come in handy.	Un couteau *pourrait* être utile

138. *think/pense*

I *think* the weather is clear.	Je *pense* que le temps est clair
I do not *think* she is here.	Je ne *pense* pas qu'elle est ici
Think before you say anything.	*pense* avant de parler

139. *free/gratuit*

The drinks come *free* with your order.	Les boissons sont *gratuites* avec la commande
Can I have this for *free?*	Puis-je avoir ça *gratuitement* ?
Today there are *free* items in the store	Aujourd'hui il y a des articles *gratuits* en boutique

140. *too/trop*

I ate *too* much.	J'ai *trop* mangé
It is *too* large.	Il est *trop* large
This is *too* bad.	C'est *trop* mauvais

141. *had/eu*

She *had* her dinner already.	Elle a déjà *eu* son diner

The boy *had* measles.	Le garçon a *eu* la rougeole
I have *had* enough.	J'en ai *eu* assez

142. *hi/salut*

Hi, I am Jill.	*Salut*, je suis Jill
The boy said *hi* to the girl.	Le garçon a dit *salut* à la fille
Hi. How was your day?	*Salut*, comment était ta journée

143. *right/raison-droite-bon*

She is always *right.*	Elle a toujours *raison*
Use your *right* hand to do the job.	Utilise ta main *droite* pour faire le travail
Jim is the *right* man for the job.	Jim est le *bon* homme pour le travail

144. *still/toujours*

I am *still* in love with her.	Je suis *toujours* amoureux d'elle
He is *still* here.	Il est *toujours* là
My hands *still* hurt.	Mes mais me font *toujours* mal

145. *system/système*

The *system* has totally malfunctioned.	Le *système* a totalement malfonctionné
This is a very unique ticketing *system.*	C'est un *système* de réservation unique

My *system* is totally fool-proof.	Mon *système* est totalement à toute épreuve

146. *after/après*

The police is *after* the crook.	La police est *après* le bandit
Please come *after* me.	S'il te plait viens *après* moi
I will eat *after* the show gets over.	Je mangerai *après* que le spectacle se termine

147. *computer/ordinateur*

Do you have a *computer* at home?	As-tu un *ordinateur* à la maison ?
My *computer* is not working.	Mon *ordinateur* ne marche pas
The *computer* has changed lives.	*L'ordinateur* a changé de vies

148. *best/meilleur*

These are his *best* works	Ce sont ses *meilleurs* travaux
Who is the *best* soccer player here?	Qui est le *meilleur* footballer ici ?
He is the *best* in his field	Il est le *meilleur* sur le terrain

149. *must/doit*

She *must* sleep right away.	Elle *doit* dormir maintenant
He *must* go.	Il *doit* partir
You *must* not fail in this subject.	Tu ne *dois* pas échouer sur ce sujet

150. *her/ses-son-lui*

Her looks are very deceptive.	Ses looks sont très trompeurs
Can I have *her* book?	Puis-je avoir son livre ?
You must give *her* some chocolates.	Tu dois *lui* donner quelques chocolats

151. *life/vie*

Her *life* is very important to me.	Sa *vie* est très importante pour moi
I will give my *life* for my nation.	Je donnerai ma *vie* pour ma nation
I have never won a lottery in my *life.*	Je n'ai jamais gangé en lotterie de ma *vie*

152. *since/depuis*

Since he is old, he walks slowly.	*Depuis* qu'il est vieux, il marche lentement
It has been raining *since* Sunday.	Il pleut *depuis* Dimanche
We have been friends ever *since.*	Nous avons été amis *depuis*

153. *could/pourrions-pourrait*

Could we have a spoon?	*Pourrions*-nous avoir une cuillère ?
Could we have a fork?	*Pourrions*-nous avoir une fourchette ?
He *could* speak French.	Il *pourrait* parler français

154. *does/est*

What *does* she have?	Qu'*est* ce qu'elle a ?
Does your dog bite?	*Est*-ce que ton chien mord ?
Where *does* it hurt?	Ou *est* ce que ça fait mal ?

155. *now/maintenant*

I am busy *now.*	Je suis occupé *maintenant*
She is out *now.*	Elle est dehors *maintenant*
I am tied up *now.*	Je suis attaché *maintenant*

156. *during/durant*

We live in England *during* summer.	Nous vivons en Angleterre *durant* l'été
I had a good time *during* Christmas.	J'ai passé du bon temps *durant* Noêl
He sleeps *during* the day.	Il dort *durant* la journée

157. *learn/apprendre*

He began to *learn* English.	Il a commencé à *apprendre* l'anglais
I want to *learn* how to swim.	Je veux *apprendre* à nager
It is never too late to *learn.*	Il n'est jamais trop tard pour *apprendre*

158. *around/autour*

He turned *around.*	Il a tourné *autour*
She looked *around.*	Elle a regardé *autour*
They walked *around.*	Ils ont marché *autour*

159. *usually/d'habitude*

Usually I am not this late.	*D'habitude* je ne suis pas aussi tardif
It rains *usually* in the afternoon.	Il pleut *d'habitude* l'après midi
Cats *usually* hate dogs.	Les chats détestent les chiens *d'habitude*

160. *form/forme*

The car's *form* is nice	La *forme* de la voiture est jolie
The player is totally out of *form*	Le joueur est totalement en baisse de *forme*
His lack of *form* is a major worry	Son manque de *forme* est un souci majeur

161. *meat/viande*

The *meat* tastes salty	La *viande* a un goût salé
The *meat* is very juicy	La *viande* est très juteuse
The *meat* is very tender.	La *viande* est très tendre

162. *air/air*

Inhale clean *air*	Inhale l'*air* pur
The *air* is dusty	L'*air* est poussiéreux
The *air* is polluted.	L'*air* est pollué

163. *day/jour*

What time of the *day* is it?	Quel moment du *jour* est-ce ?
It is a nice *day.*	C'est un beau *jour*
Run every *day.*	Courrir chaque *jour*

164. *place/lieu*

I will come to your *place.*	Je viendrai à ton *lieu*
You are in safe *place.*	Tu es en *lieu* sûr
She brought him to our *place.*	Elle l'a amené à notre *lieu*

165. *become /deviennent-devenu-devenir*

Tadpoles *become* frogs.	Les têtards *deviennent* des grenouilles
It has *become* much warmer.	C'est *devenu* plus chaud
He wishes to *become* a doctor.	Il souhaite *devenir* médecin

166. *number/numéro*

Ten is an even *number.*	Dix est un *numéro* pair
I forgot his phone *number.*	J'ai oublié son *numéro* de téléphone

Give me your cell *number.*	Donne moi ton *numéro* de téléphone

167. *public/publique-public*

The *public* memory is very short.	La mémoire *publique* est très courte
Listen to the voice of the *public.*	Ecoute la voix du *public*
The *public* reaction is very strong.	La réaction du *public* est très forte

168. *read/lis*

I always *read* from start to finish.	Je *lis* toujours du début à la fin
Do you *read* a book every week?	*Lis*-tu un livre chaque semaine ?
Do you *read* newspapers?	*Lis*-tu les journaux ?

169. *keep/garder*

I wish to *keep* this a secret.	J'espère *garder* ce secret
Keep the jewels in safe custody.	*Garde* les bijoux en sécurité
You must *keep* the documents safely.	Tu dois *garder* les documents en lieu sûr

170. *part/partie*

This *part* is totally hidden.	Cette *partie* est totalement cachée
There is another *part* of this novel.	Il y a une autre *partie* de ce roman
Enjoy his *part* in the play.	Profite de sa *partie* dans la pièce du théâtre

171. *start/démarre*

Start your day on a cheerful note.	*Démarre* ta journée sur une note joyeuse
Start the engine of the car.	*Démarre* le moteur de la voiture
Press the *start* button.	Clique sur le boutton *démarrer*

172. *year/année*

This *year* is very different.	Cette *année* est très différente
He is in second *year* of college.	Il est en seconde *année* du collège
I retired last *year.*	J'ai pris ma retraite l'*année* dernière

173. *every/chaque*

I go *every* year.	Je vais *chaque* année
Tim runs *every* day.	Tim court *chaque* jour
Study English *every* day.	Etudie l'anglais *chaque* jour

174. *field/champ*

The playing *field* is very huge.	Le *champ* du jeu est énorme
The *field* has not been properly maintained.	Le *champ* n'a pas été proprement maintenu
Come to the *field* everyday.	Viens au *champ* chaque jour

175. *large/grande*

It is too *large.*	C'est trop *grand*
We had a *large* audience.	Nous avons eu une *grande* audience
He lives in a *large* house.	Il vit dans une *grande* maison

176. *once/une fois*

You must go at *once.*	Tu dois partir en *une fois*
I *once* lived in London.	*J'ai une fois vécu à Londres*
I feed my cat *once* a day.	Je nourris mon chat *une fois* par jour

177. *available/disponible*

The book is now *available.*	Le livre est *disponible*
The DVD is *available* across all stores.	Le DVD est *disponible* dans tous les magazins
Make this book *available* to the students	Rend ce livre *disponible* à tous les étudiants

178. *down/tombée*

She went *down.*	Elle est *tombée*
Do not let him go *down.*	Ne le laisse pas *tomber*
The tree is *down.*	L'arbre est *tombé*

179. *give/abandonne-donne*

I *give* up.	J'*abandonne*
Do not *give* it to her.	Ne le lui *donne* pas
I *give* you my word.	Je te *donne* ma parole

180. *fish/poissons*

Fish keeping is a very popular hobby.	Les *poissons* doméstiques est un hobby très populaire
He can swim like a *fish.*	Il peut nager comme un *poisson*
My father caught a big *fish.*	Mon père a attrapé un gros *poisson*

181. *human/humain*

This is not at all a *human* act.	Ce n'est pas du tout un acte *humain*
Only a few *humans* could understand this	Seulement quelques *humains* peuvent comprendre ça
How can a *human* be so cruel?	Comment un *humain* peut être aussi cruel ?

182. *both/deux*

You need to call *both* of them.	Tu dois les appeler tous les *deux*
I gave you two pens. Do you have *both*?	Je t'ai donnée deux stylos. Tu as les *deux* ?
Both of us knew the answer.	Nous *deux* connaissons la réponse

183. *local/local*

You should ask the *local* boy for instructions	Tu dois demander le garçon *local* pour les instructions
The *local* language has a lot of dialects.	Le language *local* a beaucoup de dialectes
I need to learn the *local* language.	J'ai besoin d'apprendre le language *local*

184. *sure/certainement-certain*

It will rain for *sure.*	Il va *certainement* pleuvoir
Are you *sure* of your answer?	Es-tu *certain* de ta réponse ?
I am not *sure* when he will come.	Je ne suis pas *certain* quand il viendra

185. *something/quelque chose*

I should give her *something.*	Je dois lui donner *quelque chose*
Please give her *something* to eat.	S'il te plait, donne lui *quelque chose* à manger
There is *something* I need to tell you.	Il y a *quelque chose* que je dois te dire

186. *without/sans*

I cannot live *without* you.	Je ne peux pas vivre *sans* toi
You cannot live *without* water.	Tu ne peux pas vivre *sans* eau
I learnt to live *without* her.	J'ai appris à vivre *sans* elle

187. *come/viendrai-venir*

I will not *come* tomorrow.	Je ne *viendrai* pas demain
He is expected to *come* today.	Il est sensé *venir* aujourd'hui
I cannot *come* to the stadium.	Je ne peux pas *venir* au stade

188. *me/me-m'*

Would you let *me* pay?	Pourrais-tu *me* laisser payer ?
Do you hear *me?*	Tu *m'*entends ?
She knows *me.*	Elle *me* connait

189. *back/retour-rentre*

I will be *back* in 2 days.	Je serai de *retour* dans 2 jours
When will you get *back?*	Quand vas-tu *rentrer* ?
Please come *back* home soon.	S'il te plait *rentre* vite à la maison

190. *better/mieux*

You will feel *better.*	Tu te sentiras *mieux*
Tim is getting *better.*	Tim va *mieux*
Better late than never.	*Mieux* vaut tard que jamais

191. *general/général*

The *general* opinion is good	L'opinion *générale* est bonne
What is the *general* condition of your	Quel est l'état *général* de votre santé

health?	
The king, in *general,* loves all,	Le roi, en *général,* aime tout le monde

192. *process/processus*

The *process* of getting the passport is simple	Le *processus* pour obtenir le passeport est simple
Understand the *process* before moving on	Comprend le *processus* avant de passer à autre chose
Take care of the *process* before applying.	Prend soin du *processus* avant de faire la demande

193. *she/elle*

She is a bit touchy on this subject.	*Elle* est un peu sensible sur ce sujet
She is very beautiful.	*Elle* est très belle
I do not think *she* knows about it.	Je ne crois pas qu'*elle* est au courant

194. *Heat/réchauffe-chaleur*

Please *heat* up the dishes.	*Réchauffe* s'il te plait les plats
Can you feel the *heat?*	Peux-tu sentir la *chaleur*?
The *heat* is unbearable.	La *chaleur* est insupportable

195. *thanks/Merci*

Thanks for all the birthday wishes.	*Merci* pour tous les voeux

	d'anniversaire
There is no need to say *Thanks* repeatedly.	Il n'y a pas besoin de dire *merci* à maintes reprises
Thanks for waiting	*Merci* d'attendre

196. *specific/spécifique*

Please be more *specific* on this.	Sois s'il te plait plus *spécifique* sur ça
I need *specific* details about him.	J'ai besoin de détails *spécifique* à son sujet
The information is not very *specific.*	L'information n'est pas très *spécifique*

197. *enough/assez*

I have had *enough* of this.	J'ai eu *assez* de ça
I think I had eaten *enough.*	Je pensé que j'ai assez *mangé*
Do you have *enough* money in your account?	As-tu *assez* d'argent dans ton compte?

198. *long/long-longue*

The boy has *long* legs.	Le garçon a de *longues* jambes
It is a *long* story.	C'est une *longue* histoire
Her hair is very *long.*	Ses cheveux sont très *longs*

199. *lot/beaucoup*

I have a *lot* of information on this.	J'ai *beaucoup* d'information sur ça
This chapter requires a *lot* of attention.	Ce chapitre demande *beaucoup* d'information
A *lot* of crops were sold already.	*Beaucoup* de récoltes étaient déjà vendues

200. *hand/main*

The dog bit my *hand.*	Le chien a mordu ma *main*
He hurt his right *hand.*	Il a blessé sa *main* droite
The cat scratched her left *hand.*	Le chat a griffé sa *main* gauche

RANKING: 201–300
The most used words

201. Popular Populaire	202. Small Petit	203. Though Bien que	204. Experience Expérience	205. Include Inclure
206. Job Travail	207. Music Musique	208. Person Personne	209. Really Réellement	210. Although Malgré/ Même/Si
211. Thank Merci	212. Book Livre	213. Early Tôt	214. Reading Lecture	215. End Fin
216. Method Méthode	217. Never Jamais	218. Less Moins	219. Play Jouer	220. Able Peux/Peut
221. Data Donnée	222. Feel Sentir	223. High Haut	224. Off Quitter/Hors Eteint	225. Point Point
226. Type Type	227. Whether Si	228. Food Nourriture	229. Understanding Compréhension	230. Here Ici
231. Home Maison	232. Certain Certain	233. Economy Economie	234. Little Petit/Peu	235. Theory Théorie
236. Tonight Ce Soir	237. Law Loi	238. Put Mettre	239. Under Sous	240. Value Valeur
241. Always Toujours	242. Body Corps	243. Common Commun	244. Market Marché	245. Set Mis
246. Bird	247. Guide	248. Provide	249. Change	250. Interest

Oiseau	Guide	Fournir	Change	Intérêt
251. Literature Littérature	252. Sometimes Parfois	253. Problem Problème	254. Say Dire	255. Next Suivant/Près
256. Create Créer	257. Simple Simple	258. Software Logiciel	259. State Etat	260. Together Ensemble
261. Control Control	262. Knowledge Connaissance	263. Power Electricité/ Puissance	264. Radio Radio	265. Ability Compétence
266. Basic Basique	267. Course Cours	268. Economics Economie	269. Hard Dur	270. Add Ajouter
271. Company Compagnie	272. Known Connu	273. Love Amour	274. Past Passé	275. Price Prix
276. Size Taille	277. Away Loin	278. Big Grand	279. Internet Internet	280. Possible Possible
281. Television Télévision	282. Three Trois	283. Understand Comprendre	284. Various Plusieurs	285. Yourself Toi-Même
286. Card Carte	287. Difficult Difficile	288. Including Inclus	289. List Liste	290. Mind Esprit
291. Particular Particulier	292. Real Réel	293. Science Science	294. Trade Commerce	295. Consider Considérer
296. Either Aucun/ Non Plus	297. Library Bibliothèque	298. Likely Probable	299. Nature Nature	300. Fact Fait

201. *popular/populaire*

Young generation like *popular* music.	La jeune génération aime la musique *populaire*
Jim is very *popular.*	Jim est très *populaire*
Why are you so *popular?*	Pourquoi êtes-vous si *populaire*?

202. *small/petite-petit*

Her head is *small.*	Sa tête est *petite*
I only ate a *small* portion.	J'ai seulement mangé une *petite* portion
I have a *small* appetite.	J'ai un *petit* appétit

203. *though/bien que*

Even *though* he's very old, he's healthy.	*Bien qu'il* soit vieux, il a une bonne santé
She kept working even *though* she was tired.	Elle a continué à travailler *bien qu*'elle était fatiguée
She listens even *though* no one else does.	Elle écoute *bien que* personne ne le fait

204. *experience/expérience*

I have *experience* in these matters.	J'ai de *l'expérience* sur ses sujets
Do you have *experience* in this industry?	As-tu de *l'expérience* en cette industrie?

What does you *experience* tell you?	Que te dit ton *expérience*?

205. *include/inclus*

Please *include* your name here.	*Inclus* s'il te plait ton nom ici
The food is not *included* in the list.	Lerepas n'est pas *inclus* dans la liste
I did not *include* Tom's name in the squad.	Je n'ai pas *inclus* le nom de Tom dans le groupe

206. *job/travail*

The *job* is very boring.	Le *travail* est très ennuyeux
Did I get the *job?*	Ai-je obtenu le *travail*?
I am engaged in a full *job.*	Je suis engagé dans un *travail* plein

207. *music/musique*

I love *soft* music.	J'aime la *musique* douce
Loud *music* is not good for ears.	La *musique* forte n'est pas bonne pour les oreils
Turn off the music immediately.	Éteins la *musique* immédiatement

208. *person/personne*

Ask him to come in *person.*	Demande lui de venir en *personne*
That *person* looks suspicious.	Cette *personne* semble suspicieuse
Have you ever met him in *person?*	L'as-tu déjà rencontré en *personne*?

209. *really/vraiment*

I am *really* tired.	Je suis *vraiment* fatigué
I *really* like you.	Je t'aime *vraiment*
This is *really* sad.	C'est *vraiment* triste

210. *although/meme si*

I will be there *although* I may be late.	Je serai là *même si* je peux tarder
Although Tom is sick, he went to school	*Même si* Tom est malade, il est allé à l'école
Although it snowed, the traffic was normal.	*Même s'il* a neigé, le traffic était normal

211. *thank/remercier*

I *thank* God for this.	Je *remercie* dieu pour ça
Thank your stars that you are OK.	*Remercie* tes étoiles que tu vas bien
You need to *thank* your teacher.	Tu dois *remercier* ton professeur

212. *book/livre*

The *book* is very interesting.	Le *livre* est très intéressant
This *book* needs to be returned today.	Ce *livre* doit être retourné aujourd'hui
I have lost your *book.*	J'ai perdu ton *livre*

213. *early/tôt*

Go home *early.*	Va à la maison *tôt*
I need to work *early.*	Je dois travailler *tôt*
You are an *early* bird	Tu es un lève-*tôt*

214. *reading/lis*

I have been *reading* this book	Je *lis* ce livre
Are you *reading* the newspapers?	*Lis*-tu les journaux?
My teacher is *reading* the answers.	Mon professeur *lit* les réponses

215. *end/fin*

The *end* is near.	La *fin* est proche
The *end* of the movie was really good.	La *fin* du film était vraiment bonne
Can you see the *end* of this road?	Peux-tu vois la *fin* de cete route?

216. *method/méthode*

What *method* are you using for this?	Qelle *méthode* utilisez-vous pour ça?
You need to re-check your *methods.*	Tu dois revérifier tes *méthodes*
Please follow this *method* properly.	S'il te plait suis proprement cette *méthode*

217. *never/jamais*

I will *never* do this.	Je ne ferai *jamais* ça
He could *never* do this.	Il ne pourrait *jamais* faire ça
Tom has *never* heard of these things.	Tom n'a *jamais* entendu parler de ces choses

218. *less/moins*

I finished the work in *less* than an hour.	J'ai terminé le travail en *moins* d'une heure
Tom has *less* money than his brother does.	Tom a *moins* d'argent que son frère
You'll get there in *less* than ten minutes.	Tu seras là-bas en *moins* de dix minutes

219. *play/jouer*

Play it cool.	*Joue*-la tranquille
I *play* the piano.	Je *joue* au piano
I can *play* tennis.	Je peux *jouer* au tennis

220. *able/peux-peut*

I am *able* to run.	Je *peux* courir
He is *able* to ski.	Il *peut* skier
She is *able* to swim.	Elle *peut* nager

221. *data/données*

The *data* needs to be secured.	Les *données* doivent être sécurisées
Do you have any *data* on these phones?	As-tu des *données* sur ces téléphones?
I am not good at *data* crunching.	Je ne suis pas bon au traitement des *données*

222. *feel/sens*

I *feel* fine.	Je me *sens* bien
I *feel* happy.	Je me *sens* heureux
I *feel* alive.	Je me *sens* vivant

223. *high/haut*

She can jump *high*.	Elle peut sauter *haut*
The waves are *high*.	Les vagus sont *hautes*
I have a *high* fever.	J'ai une fièvre *haute*

224. *off/quitter-hors-éteint*

You should go *off*.	Tu dois *quitter*
The house is *off* limits	La maison est *hors*-limite
Turn *off* the TV.	*Éteins* la télé

225. *point/point*

She's got a *point* of view	Elle a un *point* de vue

You have a *point* there.	Tu as un *point* là
I don't see your *point.*	Je ne vois pas ton *point*

226. *type/type*

He is not my *type.*	C'est pas mon *type*
This is my *type* of things	C'est mon *type* de chose
What is your blood group *type?*	Quel est ton *type* de groupe sanguin?

227. *whether/si*

I am doubtful *whether* he will come.	Je doute *s'*il viendra
I don't know *whether* you like her or not.	Je ne sais pas *si* tu l'aimes ou pas
Do you know *whether* she can speak?	Sais-tu *si* elle peut parler?

228. *food/nourriture*

The *food* is cold	La *nourriture* est froide
We ran out of *food*	Nous sommes à court de *nourriture*
I love Italian *food.*	J'aime a *nourriture* italienne

229. *understanding/comprehension-entente*

His *understanding* is very poor	Sa *compréhension* est très faible
There is no *understanding* between them	Il n'y a pas *d'entente* entre eux

Jill has no *understanding* with his sister	Jill n'a aucune *entente* avec sa soeur

230. *here/ici*

Here we go	*Ici* nous allons
I eat *here.*	Je mange *ici*
It hurts *here.*	Ça fait mal *ici*

231. *home/maison*

I was at *home*	J'étais à la *maison*
May I go *home*?	Puis-je aller à la *maison*
She went *home.*	Elle allée à la *maison*

232. *certain/certain*

I am not *certain* about that.	Je ne sui spas *certain* de ça
Are you quite *certain* about it?	Es-tu bien *certain* de ça?
I don't know for *certain* when he will come.	Je ne sui spas *certain* quand est ce qu'il viendra

233. *economy/économie*

The *economy* of the country is in bad shape.	*L'économie* du pays est en mauvaise forme
Please understand the *economy*	S'il te plait comprend *l'économie*

No *economy* is better than ours.	Aucune *économie* n'est meilleure que la nôtre

234. *little/petit-peu*

I have a *little* sister.	J'ai une *petite* soeur
I know *little* about this.	Je sais un *peu* à ce sujet
She knows very *little* about this.	Elle sait très *peu* à ce sujet

235. *theory/théorie*

The *theory* section is very easy.	La section de *théorie* est très simple
Do you have a good *theory* on this?	As-tu une bonne *théorie* sur ça?
The Big Bang *Theory* is a hot topic now.	La *théorie* su Big Bang est un topic brûlant maintenant

236. *tonight/ce soir*

I will call him *tonight.*	Je l'appellerai *ce soir*
I will go to the match *tonight.*	J'irai au match *ce soir*
Please do not study *tonight.*	S'il te plait n'étudie pas *ce soir*

237. *law/loi*

The *law* is very strict in this country.	La *loi* est très stricte dans son pays
You are bound to respect the *law.*	Tu es tenu de respecter la *loi*
The *law* will follow you wherever you	La *loi* te poursuivra où tu iras

go	

238. *put/mets*

Put the book on the table	*Mets* le livre sur la table
Please *put* the hand in your pocket	S'il te plait *mets* la main dans ta pôche
Jill, *put* the books on the shelf	Jill, *mets* les livres sur l'étagère

239. *under/sous*

Am I *under* arrest?	Suis-je *sous* arrestation ?
I hid *under* the table.	Je me suis caché *sous* la table
Tom hid *under* the table.	Tom s'est caché *sous* la table

240. *value/valeur-valorise*

The *value* of gold has increased.	La *valeur* de l'or a augmenté
What is the *value* of these ornaments?	Quelle est la *valeur* de ces bijoux ?
I do not *value* these sentiments at all.	Je ne *valorise* pas ces sentiments du tout

241. *always/toujours*

He is *always* with me	Il est *toujours* avec moi
You're *always* singing.	Tu chantes *toujours*
Let's *always* be friends.	Soyons *toujours* amis

242. *body/corps*

My whole *body* is sore.	mon *corps* entier est douloureux
I have pains all over my *body*.	J'ai des douleurs sur tout mon *corps*
The *body*.of a mother is warm	Le *corps* d'une mère est chaud

243. *common/commun*

The dress is very *common.*	L'habit est très *commun*
What is *common* in these pictures?	Qu'y a-t-il de *commun* dans ces images ?
Do they have anything in *common?*	Ont-il quelque chose en *commun* ?

244. *market/marché*

She went to the *market* to buy vegetables.	Elle est allée au *marché* pour acheter des légumes
Karen bought a lot of things	Karen a acheté beaucoup de choses
The *market* in Singapore is huge	Le *marché* à Singapour est énorme

245. *set/mis*

Mary *set* the basket on the table.	Mary a *mis* le panier sur la able
He *set* the standards.	Il a *mis* les standards
The prisoners were *set* free.	Les prionniers étaient *mis* en liberté

246. *bird/oiseau*

This *bird* can't fly.	*L'oiseau* ne peut pas voler
I see a *bird* on the roof.	J'ai vu un *oiseau* sur le toit
I threw a stone at the *bird*.	J'ai jeté une pierre à *l'oiseau*

247. *guide/guide*

The *guide* was very honest.	Le *guide* était très honnête
I need a good *guide* to travel	J'ai besoin d'un bon *guide* pour voyager
The boy acted as a *guide* to the tourists.	Le garçon a agi comme un *guide* aux touristes

248. *provide/fournir*

Please *provide* some food.	S'il te plait *fournis* quelque nourriture
Can you *provide* a bill?	Peux-tu *fournir* une facture ?
Please *provide* a towel today.	S'il te plait *fourni* une serviette aujourd'hui

249. *change/change*

Don't *change* the subject.	Ne *change* pas le sujet
Fashions *change* quickly.	La mode *change* vite
I *change* my mind a lot.	Je *change* mon avis beaucoup

250. *interest/intérêt*

What would be the total *interest* on loan?	Quel qerait *l'intérêt* total du prêt ?
I do not have any *interest* in these matters.	Je n'ai aucun *intérêt* à ces sujets
Please show some *interest* in the matter.	S'il te plait montre un peu *d'intérêt* à ce sujet

251. *literature/litérature*

She does not like English *literature.*	Elle n'aime pas la *littérature* anglaise
Do you like the russian *literature*	Aimes-tu la *littérature* russe ?
You must score high in *literature.*	tu dois obtenir une bonne note en *littérature*

252. *sometimes/parfois*

We *sometimes* see them.	On les vois *parfois*
We *sometimes* meet them.	On les rencontre *parfois*
Dreams *sometimes* come true.	Les rêves deviennent *parfois* réalité

253. *problem/problème*

One million people have this *problem.*	Un millon de personnes ont ce *problème*
Acne is a *problem* for young people.	L'acné est un *problème* pour les jeunes
He has a *problem* of huge proportions.	Il a un *problème* de grandes proportions

254. *say/dira-dis*

He will not *say* yes.	Il ne *dira* pas oui
What did you *say*?	Qu'a –tu *dis* ?
What did she *say*?	Qu'a-t'elle *dit* ?

255.*next/près-prochain*

She sat *next* to me.	Elle s'est asssise *près* de moi
Check back *next* week	Contrôle la semaine *prochaine*
May I sit *next* to you?	Puis-je m'assoire *près* de toi ?

256. *create/créer*

I need to *create* a proper wordsheet.	Je dois *créer* une feuille de travail propre
Can you *create* a sandcastle?	Peux-tu *créer* un château de sable ?
I must *create* a presentation quickly	Je dois *créer* une présentation rapidement

257. *simple/simple*

The girl looks very *simple.*	La fille semble très *simple*
I have very *simple* aspirations in life.	J'ai de très *simples* aspirations dans la vie
This questions are very *simple.*	Ces questions sont très *simples*

258. *software/logiciel*

Does your laptop have the latest *software?*	Est-ce que ton ordinateur a le dernier *logiciel* ?
I need an updated version of the *software*	J'ai besoin d'un version à jour du *logiciel*
Can I borrow this *software?*	Puis-je emprunter ce *logiciel* ?

259. *state/état*

The *state* of affairs is in total disarray.	*L'état* des affaires est en total désordre
I have a fragile *state* of mind.	J'ai un *état* d'esprit fragile
¿Which *state* do you come from?	De quel *Etat* viens-tu ?

260. *together/ensemble*

Get your things *together.*	Range tes affaires *ensemble*
Let's get *together* tomorrow	Allons *ensemble* demain
They agreed to work *together.*	Il ont convenu de travailler *ensemble*

261. *control/contrôler*

Nobody can control us.	Personne ne peut nous *contrôler*
Tom couldn't *control* his anger.	Tom ne peut pas *contrôler* sa colère
I wish I could *control* my appetite.	J'espère pouvoir *contrôler* mon appétit

262. *knowledge/connaissance*

My *knowledge* in this field is very	Ma *connaissance* sur ce champ est très

limited.	limitée
Do you have any *knowledge* about this?	As-tu des *connaissances* sur ce sujet
You have good general *knowledge.*	Tu as une bonne *connaissance* générale

263. *power/électricité-puissance*

The storm caused a *power* outage.	La tempête a causé une panne *d'électricité*
What will happen if there's *power* failure?	Qu'arrivera t'il s'il y a une panne *d'électricité* ?
I need will *power* to loose weight	J'ai besoin de la *puissance* de volonté pour perdre du poids

264. *radio/radio*

Did you hear the news on the *radio*?	As-tu entendu les infos à la *radio* ?
Turn off the *radio*, please.	Eteins la *radio* s'il te plait
I'm listening to the *radio.*	J'écoute la *radio*

265. *ability/compétence*

He has the *ability* to make a good plan.	Il a la *compétence* pour faire un bon plan
Do you have the required *ability*?	As-tu la *compétence* requise ?
I have very limited *ability.*	J'ai une *compétence* très limitée

266. *basic/basique*

Please advise the *basic* details	Donne s'il te plait les détails *basiques*
The features of the phone are very *basic.*	Les options du téléphone sont très *basiques*
Do you have any *basic* idea about this?	As-tu une idée *basique* sur ça ?

267. *course/cours*

After the *course* she can speak English.	Après le *cours* elle peut parler Anglais
You need a *course* to learn golf	Tu as besoin d'un *cours* pour apprendre le gold
The *course* is 5 days long	Le *cours* est de 5 jours

268. *economics/economie*

She had no idea about *economics* matters.	Elle n'a aucune idée sur *l'économie*
The boy failed in *economics.*	Le garçon a échoué en *économie*
You need to understand first the *economics*	Tu dois comprendre *l'économie* de base

269. *hard/dur*

He tries *hard.*	Il essaie *dur*
She worked *hard.*	Elle travaille *dur*
She hit him *hard.*	Il l'a frappé *dur*

270. *add/ajouter*

You need to *add* up all these.	Tu dois *ajouter* tous ceux-là
Please *add* up the total bills.	*Ajoute* s'il te plait les factures totales
How much did you *add* here?	Combien as-tu *ajouté* ici ?

271. *company/compagnie*

She quit the *company.*	Elle a quitté la *comapgnie*
Charge this to my *company.*	Mettez ça à la charge de ma *compagnie*
That *company* went bankrupt.	Cette *compagnie* a fait faillite

272. *known/connu*

He is *known* to everyone.	Il est *connu* de tout le monde
I have *known* him a long time.	Je l'ai *connu* longtemps
She's well *known* as a singer.	Elle est bien *connue* comme une chanteuse

273. *love/aimons-aimait-amour*

We *love* each other.	Nous nous *aimons*
He used to *love* her.	Il *l'aimait*
I like *love* stories.	J'aime les histoires *d'amour*

274. *past /passé*

Don't worry about the *past.*	Ne te préoccupe pas du *passée*
I don't care about your *past.*	Je me fiche de ton *passé*
It's almost half *past* eleven.	La moitié de 11h est *passé*

275. *price/prix*

The *price* of eggs is going up.	Le *prix* des œufs a augmenté
Does that *price* include tax?	Est-ce que ce *prix* inclut la taxe ?
They agreed on a *price.*	Il ont convenu d'un *prix*

276. *size/taille*

He is about my *size.*	Il a ma *taille*
Do you have jeans in my *size*?	As-tu des jean à ma *taille* ?
Mi size in much bigger	Ma *taille* est bien plus grande

277. *away/loin*

I was crying while you were *away.*	Je pleurais quand tu étais *loin*
Send Jim *away.*	Envoie Jim *loin*
He is *away* on business.	Il est *loin* en affaires

278. *big/grande-grands*

The house is very *big.*	La maison est très *grande*
He has three *big* dogs.	Il a trois *grands* chiens

I have three *big* beds in my home.	J'ai trois *grands* lits dasn ma maison

279. *internet/internet*

The *internet* is not working properly.	*L'internet* ne marche pas correctement
The *internet* speed is not good at all.	La vitesse *d'internet* n'est pas bonne du tout
Do you have *internet* at home?	As-tu *internet* à la maison ?

280. *possible/posible*

She is asking how that is *possible.*	Elle demande comment est-ce *possible.*
All of us want to live as long as *possible.*	Nous tous voulons vivre le plus longtemps *possible*
I will talk to him, if *possible.*	Je lui parlerai, si *possible*

281. *television/télévision*

The *television* set is working properly.	La *télévision* fonctionne correctement
Please switch on the *television.*	Allume s'il te plait la *télévision*
The *television* sets need to be changed	La *télévision* doit être changée

282. *three/trois*

He has *three* sons.	Il a *trois* enfants
I have *three* dogs.	J'ai *trois* chiens
The desk has *three* drawers.	Le bureau a *trois* tiroirs

283. *understand/comprendre*

I think I *understand.*	Je pense *comprendre*
Do you *understand* German?	*Comprends*-tu l'allemand ?
I could hardly *understand* him.	Je peux difficielement le *comprendre*

284. *various/plusieurs*

We talked about *various* topics.	Nous avons parlé de *plusieurs* sujets
There are *various* kinds of coffee.	Il ya *plusieurs* types de café
Various kinds of toys are available.	*Plusieurs* types de jouets sont disponibles

285. *yourself/toi-même*

Do it by *yourself.*	Fais-le *toi-même*
Believe in *yourself.*	Crois en *toi-même*
Try it out *yourself.*	Essaie-le *toi-même*

286. *card/carte*

He sent a *card* to Mary.	Il a envoyé une *carte* à Mary
Can I use the credit *card?*	Puis-je utiliser la *carte* de crédit ?
He sent me a birthday *card.*	Il m'a envoyé une *carte* d'anniversaire

287. *difficult/difficile*

It is *difficult* to understand her problem.	Il est *difficile* de comprendre son problème
The exam was very *difficult.*	L'examen était très *difficile*
Winning the league would be very *diffcult.*	Gagner le championnat serait très *difficile*

288. *including/inclus*

Is the hotel bill *including* taxes?	Est-ce que la facture d'hôtel *inclut* les taxes ?
I am *including* her name in the list.	*J'inclus* son nom dans la liste
Including me in the team made me proud.	*M'inclure* dans le groupe me rend fier

289. *list/liste*

I added his name to the *list.*	J'ai ajouté son nom à la *lsite*
Please add my name to the *list.*	S'il te plait ajoute mon nom à la *liste*
Here is a *list* of things you need on that day.	Voici une *liste* des choses dont tu auras besoin ce jour

290. *mind/esprit*

Your *mind* is brilliant	Votre *esprit* est brillant
No *mind* can stand this ill treatment	Aucun *esprit* ne peut supporter ce

	traitement malade
Mind matters	*L'esprit* importe

291. *particular/particulier*

My father is very *particular* about food.	Mon père est très *particulier* sur la nourriture
I do not want to go anywhere in *particular.*	Je ne veux aller nulle part en *particulier*
I want to emphasize this point in *particular.*	Je vous souligner ce poit en *particulier*

292. *real/réelles-réels*

The stories seemed so *real.*	Les histoires semblent *réelles*
The stuffed animals look very *real.*	Les animaux en peluche semblent *réels*
Do you think the horror pictures are *real?*	Crois-tu que les images d'horreur sont *réelles* ?

293. *science/science*

Science has made our life simpler.	La *science* a rendu notre vie plus facile
Why did you fail in the *science* subjects?	Pourquoi as-tu échoué dans les sujets de *sciences* ?
Do you have *science* as one of the subjects?	As-tu les *sciences* comme l'un des sujets ?

294. *trade/commerce*

The *trade* agreements are not trustworthy.	Les accords *commerciaux* ne sont pas fiables
There is a *trade* strike today.	Il y a une grève de *commerce* aujourd'hui
Where do you play your *trade?*	Ou exerces-tu ton *commerces* ?

295. *consider/considère*

I *consider* him to be an excellent teacher.	Je le *considère* comme un excellent professeur
She urged me to *consider* the request.	Elle m'a exhorté de *considérer* la demande
Please *consider* my proposal.	S'il vous plait *considérez* ma proposition

296. *either/aucun-non plus*

I do not know *either* of them.	Je ne connais *aucun* d'eux
I cannot comprehend it *either.*	Je ne peux pas le comprendre *non plus*
I do not like it, *either.*	Je ne l'aime pas, *non plus*

297. *library/bibliotèque*

They have access to the *library.*	Il ont accès à la *bibliotèque*
I left my books in the *library.*	J'ai laissé mes livres à la *bibliotèque*
We live near a big *library.*	On habite à côté d'une grande

	bibliothèque

298. *likely/probable*

The sky is *likely* to clear up.	Il est *probable* que le ciel est clair
He is *likely* to be fine.	Il est *probable* qu'il soit bien
He is *likely* to come.	Il est *probable* qu'il vienne

299. *nature/nature*

I don't like the *nature* of the child.	Je n'aime pas la *nature* de l'enfant
It was in his *nature.*	C'était dans sa *nature*
Nature can be wild.	La *nature* peut être sauvage

300. *fact/fait*

This is based on *fact*	C'est basé sur des *faits*
I cannot hide this *fact*	Je ne peux pas cacher ce *fait*
This *fact* cannot be denied	Ce *fait* ne peut pas être nié

RANKING: 301–300
The most used words

301. Line Ligne	302. Product Produit	303. Care Soin	304. Group Groupe	305. Idea Idée
306. Risk Risque	307. Several Plusieurs	308. Someone Quelqu'un	309. Temperature Température	310. United Unis
311. Word Mot/Parole	312. Fat Gros	313. Force Force	314. Key Clé	315. Light Lumière
316. Simply Simple	317. Today Aujourd' Hui	318. Training Formation	319. Until Jusqu'à	320. Major Majeur
321. Name Nom	322. Personal. Personnel	323. School Ecole	324. Top Haut	325. Current Actuel
326. Generally Généralement	327. Historical Historique	328. Investment Investissement	329. Left Gauche	330. National National
331. Amount Montant	332. Level Niveau	333. Order Ordre	334. Practice Pratique	335. Research Recherche
336. Sense Sens	337. Service Service	338. Area Secteur	339. Cut Couper/ Rédiction	340. Hot Chaud
341. Instead A La Place	342. Least Moins	343. Natural Naturel	344. Physical Physique	345. Piece Pièce
346.	347.	348.	349.	350.

Show Spectacle	Society Société	Try Essayer	Check Vérifier	Choose Choisir
351. Develop Développer	352. Second Second	353. Useful Utile	354. Web Web/Toile	355. Activity Activité
356. Boss Chef	357. Short Court	358. Story Histoire	359. Call Appeler	360. Industry Industrie
361. Last Dernier	362. Media Presse	363. Mental Psychiatrique mental	364. Move Bouger	365. Pay Payer
366. Sport Sport	367. Thing Chose	368. Actually Actualité	369. Against Contre	370. Far Loin
371. Fun Amuser	372. House Maison	373. Let Laisse	374. Page Page	375. Remember Souviens
376. Term Terme	377. Test Test	378. Within Dans	379. Along Avec moi	380. Answer Réponse
381. Increase Augmenter	382. Oven Four	383. Quite Tout a fait/ Complètement	384. Scared Peur	385. Single Seul
386. Sound Son	387. Again Encore	388. Community Communauté	389. Definition Définition	390. Focus Concentration
391. Individual Individuel/ Individu	392. Matter Problème	393. Safety Sécurtié	394. Turn Tourne Tournure	395. Everything Tout
396. Kind	397. Quality	398. Soil	399. Ask	400. Board

Gentil Type	Qualité	Sol	Demander	Bord

301. *line/ligne*

Wait in *line,* please	Reste en *ligne*, s'il te plait
Write on every other *line*	Ecris sur toute autre *ligne*
Please waite in *line* for a moment	Restez en *ligne* s'il vous plait pour un moment

302. *product/produit*

The product is really good.	Le *produit* est très bon
Do you have any other *product?*	As-tu d'autres *produits* ?
This *product* is very expensive.	Ce *produit* est très cher

303. *care/soin*

Do take *care* of him.	Prend *soin* de lui
I am going to take *care* of him.	Je vais prendre *soin* de lui
Please do take *care* of yourself.	S'il te plait prend *soin* de toi

304. *group/groupe*

The *group* of strangers is coming this way.	Un *groupe* d'étrangers vers par ici
I saw an odd *group* there.	J'ai vu un *groupe* bizarre là-bas

It is a huge *group.*	C'est un grand *groupe*

305. *idea/idée*

I had no *idea.*	Je n'ai aucune *idée*
Do you have any *idea* about this?	As-tu une *idée* à ce sujet ?
He always comes up with an *idea.*	Il vient toujours avec une *idée*

306. *risk/risque*

There is no *risk* in this business.	Il n'y a pas de *risque* dans cette affaire
I will not take this *risk.*	Je ne prendrai pas ce *risque*
She takes too many *risks.*	Elle prend trop de *risque*

307. *several/plusieurs*

He came *several* times	Il est venu *plusieurs* fois
I have been abroad *several* times	J'ai été à l'étranger *plusieurs* fois
I have been there on *several* occasions	J'ai été là-bas à *plusieurs* occasions

308. *someone/quelqu'un*

Someone is at the door.	*Quelqu'un est à la porte*
I heard *someone* whistle.	J'ai entendu *quelqu'un* siffler
Please ask *someone* else.	S'il te plait demande à *quelqu'un* d'autre

309. *temperature/température*

My *temperature* is normal.	Ma *température* est normale
I seem to have a *temperature.*	Je crois que j'ai une *température*
My mother took my *temperature.*	Ma mère a pris ma *température*

310. *united/unis*

We are always *united*	Nous sommes toujours *unis*
Both teams *united* for the parade	Les deux équipes *unies* pour la parade
The brothers should be *united*	Les frères doivent êtres *unis*

311. *word/mot-parole*

Please read every *word* in the document.	Lis s'il te plait chaque *mot* dans ce document
You didn't keep your *word.*	Tu n'as pas tenu ta *parole*
I give you my *word.*	Je donne ma *parole*

312. *fat/gros*

I am very *fat.*	Je suis très *gros*
Je suis extrêmement gros	Je suis extrêmement *gros*
Do you think I am *fat?*	Penses-tu que je suis *gros* ?

313. *force/force*

Tom was *forced* to make a hasty	Tom était *forcé* de prendre une

decision.	décision rapide
I was *forced* to exclude him.	J'étais *forcé* de l'exclure
Please do not *force* her.	S'il te plait ne la *force* pas

314. *key/clé*

I lost my car *key.*	J'ai perdu ma *clé* de voiture
Do you have the *key* to this door?	As-tu la *clé* de cette porte ?
Where is the *key* to the wardrobe?	Où est la *clé* de ce placard ?

315. *light/lumière*

The *light* is on.	La *lumière* est allumée
Put out the *light.*	Eteins la *lumière*
Turn *off* the light.	Eteins la *lumière*

316. *simply/simplement*

I *simply* don't know.	Je ne sais *simplement* pas
She was *simply* available	Elle était *simplement* disponible
I can *simply* marry him.	Je peux *simplement* me marier avec lui

317. *today/aujourd'hui*

What day is *today?*	Quel jour est *aujourd'hui* ?
I need to see her *today.*	Je dois la voir *aujourd'hui*

I lost my mom *today.*	J'ai perdi ma mère *aujourd'hui*

318. *training/formation*

My *training* is not yet complete.	Ma *formation* n'est pas encore terminée
You will be sent back to *training* .	Tu seras renvoyé en *formation*
You lack proper *training.*	Tu manque une vraie *formation*

319. *until/jusqu'à*

We talked *until* two.	Nous avons parlé *jusqu'à* deux heures
I will stay here *until* ten.	Je resterai *jusqu'à* 10 heures
Wait *until* further notice.	Attends *jusqu'à* nouvel avis

320. *major/majeur*

What are your *major* subjects?	Quels sont tes sujets *majeurs* ?
A *major* success would helped	Un succès *majeur* aiderait
The boy didn´t get a major harm.	Le garçon n'a pas de blessure *majeure*

321. *name/nom*

What is your *name?*	Quel est ton *nom* ?
You have a very sweet *name.*	Tu as un *nom* très doux

I will name this building after you.	Je nommerai ce batiment en ton *nom*

322. *personal/personnel*

This is a very *personal* matter.	C'est un problème très *personnel*
I keep my *personal* items in the bag.	Je garde mes objets *personnels* dans le sac
Please come for the *personal* interview.	Venez s'il vous plait pour l'entretien *personnel*

323. *school/école*

The *school* will be closed tomorrow.	*L'école* sera fermée demain
When will your *school* open?	Quand ouvrira votre *école*
I do not like going to *school.*	Je n'aime pas aller à *l'école*

324. *top/haut*

She wants to reach the *top.*	Elle veut aller *haut*
He lives at the *top* of the hill.	Il vit en *haut* de la colline
This book goes on the top shelf.	Ce livre va à l'étagère du *haut*

325. *current/actuel*

What is the *current* scenario?	Quel est le scénario *actuel* ?
The *current* profile is not fully updated.	Le profil *actuel* n'est pas complétement à jour

The *current* situation is pretty bad.	La situation *actuelle* est très mauvaise

326. *generally/généralement*

Generally, I don't speak like this.	*Généralement,* je ne parle pas comme ça
What do you do *generally?*	Que fais-tu *généralement* ?
There has been a lot of confusion *generally.*	Il y a eu beaucoup de confusion *généralement*

327. *historical/historique*

This place has a *historical* significance.	Le lieu a une signification *historique*
I love visiting *historical* places.	J'aime visiter les lieux *historiques*
Are there any *historical* attractions?	Y a-t-il une attraction *historique* ?

328. *investment/investissement*

Your *investment* would be welcome	Ton *investissement* serait le bienvenu
Goodness is a good *investment*	La bonté est un bon *investissement*
I always believe in a good *investment.*	Je crois toujours en un bon *investissement*

329. *left/ gauche*

I was standing on the *left* side	je me tenais du côté *gauche*
I do everything with my *left* hand	Je fais tout avec ma main *gauche*

The *left* corner is wrong	Le coin *gauche* est faux

330. *national/national*

I have a sense of *nation* duty.	J'ai un sens du devoir *national*
The *nation* integrity is very important.	L'integrité *nationale* est très importante
He performed his *nation* duties with pride.	Il a accompli ses devoirs *nationaux* avec fierté

331. *amount/montant-quantité*

The *amount* is very little	Le *montant* et très petit
He amassed a huge *amount* of wealth	Il a amassé une énorme *quantité* de richesse
Do you have that *amount* with you?	As-tu ce *montant* avec toi ?

332. *level/niveau*

We will talk to high *level* authorities.	Nous parlerons aux autorités de haut *niveau*
This game has only one *level.*	Ce jeu a seulement un *niveau*
I need to increase my *level* of attention.	Je dois améliorer mon *niveau* de concentration

333. *order/ordre*

He put his room in *order.*	Il a mis sa chambre en *ordre*

Everything is in *order*	Tout est en *ordre*
Order is essential for prosperity	*L'ordre* est essentiel pour la prospérité

334. *practice/pratique*

You need to *practice* hard.	Tu dois *pratiquer* dur
Practice the numerical exercises.	*Pratique* les exercices numériques
The *practice* sessions were long.	Les sessions *pratiques* étaient longues

335. *research/recherche*

A complete *research* is required	Une *recherche* complète est requise
My *research* papers are lost.	Mes papiers de *recherche* sont perdus
Did you do your *research* properly?	As-tu fais proprement ta *recherche* ?

336. *sense/sens*

He has lost his common *sense.*	Il a perdu son *sens* commun
He regained his *sense* after a while.	Il a retroué son *sens* après un moment
Do you have any *sense* of all these?	As-tu un *sens* de tous ceux-là ?

337. *service/service*

I have been in *service* for 3 years.	J'étais en *service* pendant 3 ans
The cell phone is out of *service.*	Le téléphone est hors *service*
The car needs to go to the *service*	La voiture doit aller à la station *service*

station.	

338. *area/secteur*

The *area* is very developed.	Le *secteur* est très développé
Clean this *area* first.	Néttoie d'abord le *secteur*
The whole area is taken care of	Tout le *secteur* est protégé

339. *cut/coupure-réduction-coupent*

I have a deep *cut.*	J'ai une *coupure* profonde
There has been a pay *cut.*	Il y a eu une *réduction* du salaire
These scissors *cut* well.	Ces ciseaux *coupent* bient

340. *hot/chaud*

It is *hot* today.	Il fait *chaud* aujourd'hui
The room is *hot.*	La chambre est *chaude*
Tom likes *hot* curry.	Tom aime le curry *chaud*

341. *instead/au lieu-à la place*

Instead of him, I will go	*A sa place*, j'irai
Please feed her *instead.*	Nourris la s'il teplait *à la place*
Work *instead* of sitting idle.	Travaille *au lieu* de rester inactif

342. *least/moins*

I can walk at *least* two miles.	Je peux marcher au *moins* 2 miles
He has the *least* money of us all.	Il a le *moins* d'argent de nous tous
I feed him at *least* once a week.	Je le nourris au *moins* une fois par semaine

343. *natural/naturel*

The fruit juice is 100% *natural.*	Le jus de fruit est 100% *naturel*
Natural hot spring water is healthy	L'eau de source chaude *naturelle* est saine
This is a *natural* garden.	C'est un jardin *naturel*

344. *physical/physique*

Let us not get to the *physical* level	Ne passons pas au stade *physique*
Please do some *physical* exercises	Fais s'il teplait quelques exercices *physiques*
The relationship got *physical*	La relation est devenue *physique*

345. *piece/pièce*

That was the last *piece* of cake.	C'était la dernière *pièce* du gâteau
I want a *piece* of candy.	Je veux un *pièce* de bonbon
Jim got a small *piece* of pie.	Jim a eu une petite *pièce* de tarte

346. *show/spectacle*

Did you watch the full *show?*	As-tu vu tout le *spectacle* ?
There is an evening *show* every day.	Il y a un *spectacle* de soir chaque jour
She did go to the *show*	Elle est partie au *spectacle*

347. *society/société*

Please keep the *society* out of this.	Laisse s'il te plait la *société* hors de ça
The *society* was aware of all.	La *société* était au courant de tout
The *society* will never approve of this.	La *société* n'approuvera jamais ça

348. *try/essayer-essaie*

You must *try*	Tu dois *essayer*
Try till you succeed.	*Essaie* jusqu'à ce que tu réussis
You did not *try* hard enough.	Tu n'as pas *essayé* assez dur

349. *check/vérifier*

Please *check* your belongings.	*Vérifie* s'il te plait tes biens
You need to *check* the bill.	Tu dois *vérifier* la facture
Check the rooms before you leave.	*Vérifie* les chambres avec que tu partes

350. *choose/choisir*

Choose the shirt you prefer	*Choisis* la chemise que tu préfères
Choose the one you like	*Choisis* celui que tu aimes

Please *choose* one person	*Choisis* s'il te plait une personne

351. *develop/développer*

I will *develop* software next month	Je *développerai* un logiciel le mois prochain
You need to *develop* your vocabulary.	Tu dois *développer* ton vocabulaire
Jill has to *develop* her body to compete	Jill doit *développer* son corps pour concourir

352. *second/seconde*

Give me a *second!* I will come back.	Donne moi une *seconde*! Je reviendrai
You are just a *second* late for the interview.	Tu est en retard d'une *seconde* pour l'entretien
Wait a *second!* I am coming.	Attends une *seconde*! J'arrive

353. *useful/utile*

This tool had been very *useful.*	Cet outil a été très *utile*
Iron is a *useful* metal	L'acier est un métal *utile*
The man gave a *useful* piece of advice.	L'homme a donné un conseil *utile*

354. *web/ web-toile*

It is actually a *web* based company.	C'est une compagnie basée sur le *web*
The spiders are known for their *webs.*	Les araignées sont connues pour leurs

	toiles
You have entered a *web* of complexities.	Tu es entrée dans une *toile* de complexités

355. *activity/activité*

Engage yourself in any sort of *activity.*	Engage-toi dans n'importe quelle sorte *d'activité*
Their *activity* is very expensive	Leur *activité* est très chère
These documents relate to that *activity*	Ces document se rapportent à cette *activité*

356. *boss/chef*

The *boss* was very angry at Jim.	Le *chef* était très en colère après jim
Please inform your *boss.*	Informe ton *chef* s'il te plait
The *boss* will never agree to this.	Le *chef* n'approuvera jamais ça

357. *short/court*

The girl had *short* hair.	La fille a des cheuveux *courts*
The tie is very *short.*	La cravate est très *courte*
Why do you always wear *short* pants?	Pourquoi portes-tu toujours un pantalon *court* ?

358. *story/histoire*

What is the moral of the *story?*	Quelle est la morale de *l'histoire* ?
Tell me a horror *story*	Raconte moi une *histoire* d'horreur
Do you have any *story* book?	As-tu un livre *d'histoire* ?

359. *call/appeler*

The doctor will be *called*	Le médecin sera *appelé*
Please *call* the police.	*Appelle* s'il te plait la police
I need to *call* my friend.	Je dois *appeler* mon ami

360. *industry/industrie*

There is a strike in the *industry* today	Il y a un grève dans *l'industrie* aujourd'hui
There is no future in the textile *industry.*	Il n'y a aucun avenir dans *l'industrie* du textile
The oil *industry* is very rich	*L'industrie* du pétrole est très riche

361. *last/dernier*

Jim stood *last* in the history test.	Jim est arrivé *dernier* dans le test d'histoire
I was the *last* one to enter the reception.	J'étais le *dernier* à entrer dans la réception
Have the *last* piece of cake.	Prends la *dernière* pièce du gâteau

362. *media/presse*

The *media* room was full of people	La salle de *presse* était remplie de gens
Don not talk to the *media.*	Ne parle pas à la *presse*
The *media* people are very irritating.	Les gens de *presse* sont très irritants

363. *mental/psychiatrique-mental*

The *mental* hospital is located 50 miles away	L'hopital *psychiatrique* est à 50 miles plus loin
His *mental* condition is not okay.	Sa condition *mentale* n'est pas bonne
The doctor is seeing *mental* patients.	Le médecin voit des malades *mentaux*

364. *move/bouger*

I need to *move* from here.	Je dois *bouger* d'ici
Please *move* from my line of sight.	*Bouge* s'il te plait de ma ligne de visée
The dog will *move* when the car starts	Le chien *bougera* quand la voiture démarre

365. *pay/paierai-paie*

I will *pay* the invoice next week.	Je *paierai* la facture la semaine prochaine
Please *pay* in cash.	*Paie* s'il te plait en espèces
Always *pay* in local currency.	*Paie* toujours en devise locale

366. *sport/sport*

Cricket is the most loved *sport* in UK	Le Cricket et le *sport* le plus aimé au Royaume-Uni
Jill does not like any *sport* at all.	Jill n'aime aucun *sport* du tout
Soccer is the most popular *sport* in Europa	Le Football est le *sport* le plus populaire ne Europe

367. *thing/chose*

What is that *thing?*	C'est quoi cette *chose* ?
There is no such *thing* here.	Il n'y a pas de telle *chose* ici
Do not bring this *thing* to class.	N'apporte pas cette *chose* en classe

368. *actually/au fait*

The party was *actually* for him.	La fête était *au fait* pour lui
He *actually* looked very sympathetic.	Il semble *au fait* très sympathique
I *actually* forgot her birthday.	J'ai *au fait* oublié son anniversaire

369. *against/contre*

He was always *against* me.	Il était toujours *contre* moi
This is *against* the rules.	C'est *contre* les règles
Do not speak *against* me.	Ne parle pas *contre* moi

370. *far/loin*

The house is very *far* from here.	La maison est très *loin* d'ici

How *far* is this place?	Combien est *loin* cette place ?
It cannot be very *far* from here.	Ça ne peut pas être plus *loin* d'ici

371. *fun/amusant-amuse*

Where is the *fun* element here?	Où est l'élément *amusant* ici ?
There is no *fun* in this show	Il n'y a rien *d'amusant* dans le spectacle
Please have *fun* in the party	*Amuse*-toi s'il te plait à la fête

372. *house/maison*

The *house* seems to be haunted.	La *maison* semble être hantée
Look at the *house* in the corner!	Regarde la *maison* au coin
There is someone in the *house.*	Il y a quelqu'un dans la *maison*

373. *let/laisser*

You cannot *let* everybody come in.	Tu ne peux pas *laisser* tout le monde entrer
Please *let* me in.	*Laisse*-moi entrer s'il te plait
Do not *let* him play here.	Ne le *laisse* pas jouer ici

374. *page/page*

Turn the *page.*	Tourne la *page*
The candle fell on the *page.*	La bougie est tombé sur la *page*

You must start writing a fresh *page.*	Tu dois commencer à écrire une nouvelle *page*

375. *remember/souvenir*

I cannot *remember* the facts	Je ne peux pas me *souvenir* des faits
Do you *remember* me after so long?	Te *souviens*-tu de moi après si longtemps ?
Remember to pay the bills on time.	*Souviens*-toi de payer les facture à temps

376. *term/ terme*

Will you comply with the terms?	Te conformeras-tu aux *termes* ?
This is the end of the second *term.*	C'est la fin du second *terme*
I do not think his *term* is over	Je ne pense pas que son *terme* est fini

377. *test/test*

We have a physics *test* tomorrow.	Nous avons des *tests* physiques de main
You need to have a blood *test.*	Tu dois avoir un *test* sanguin
The teacher announced a surprise *test* today.	Le professeur a annoncé un *test* surprise demain

378. *within/dans*

I live *within* 2 km of the station.	J'habite *dans* 2 km de la station

She cremated *within* 24 hours	Elle est incinérée *dans* 24 heures
Within one month, he will go back	*Dans* un mois, il sera de retour

379. *along/avec*

He gets *along* with me.	Il va *avec* moi
Come *along* with me.	Viens *avec* moi
Do bring her *along* with me so I may see her	Amène la *avec* moi pour que je puisse la voir

380. *answer/réponse*

There is no *answer* to such questions.	Il n'y a pas de *réponse* à de telles questions
I do not have an *answer* for this.	Je n'ai pas de *réponse* pour ça
Please *answer* correctly.	*Réponds* correctement s'il te plait

381. *increase/augmentation-augmenter*

There will be an *increase* in the interest rate	Il y aura une *augmentation* du taux d'intérêt
Your height will *increase* with these pills.	Ta taille continue *d'augmenter* avec ces comprimés
Please *increase* my remuneration.	*Augmente* s'il te plait ma rémunération

382. *oven/four*

Please put the cake in the *oven.*	Mets s'il te plait le gâteau dans le *four*
The *oven* needs repairing.	Le *four* a besoin de réparation
We need to buy a new *oven.*	Nous devons acheter un nouveau *four*

383. *quite/tout à fait-complétement*

This is not *quite* true.	Ce n'est pas *tout à fait* vrai
I am *quite* sure.	Je suis *tout à fait* sûr
This is *quite* noisy	C'est *complétement* bruyant

384. *scared/peur*

I am *scared* to death.	J'ai *peur* de mourir
He is very *scared* after the incident.	Il a *peur* après l'accident
Don't be so *scared.*	N'aie pas *peur*

385. *single/seul*

Why are you still *single?*	Pourqioi es-u toujours *seul* ?
He remained *single* all his life.	Il est resté *seul* toute sa vie
She failed to understand a *single* word.	Elle n'a pas compris un *seul* mot

386. *sound/son*

The boys made a loud *sound.*	Les enfants émettent un *son* fort
The *sound* of the doors awakened me.	Le *son* des portes m'a réveillé

Please, turn down that *sound.*	Baisse s'il te plait ce *son*

387. *again/encore*

I will never do this *again*	Je ne ferai jamais ça *encore*
He committed the same mistake *again*	Il a *encore* commis la même erreur
Please come to my house *again*	Viens *encore* s'il te plait à ma maison

388. *community/communauté*

The *community* college is good.	Le collège de la *communauté* est bien
Please give the donation to the *community*	Donne s'il te plait le don à la *communauté*
There is an ill-feeling in the *community.*	Il y a un sentiment malsain dans la *communauté*

389. *definition/definition*

You gave a wrong *definition.*	Tu as donné la mauvaise *définition*
Please write the *definition* of the words	Ecris s'il te plait al *définition* des mots
The definition of the term has changed	La *définition* du terme a changé

390. *focus/concentration-concentre*

You should never lose your *focus.*	Tu ne dois jamais perdre ta *concentration*
The player lost his *focus* on the match.	Le joueur a perdu sa *concentration*

	dans le match
If you *focus* you will achieve success.	Si tu te *concentres* tu réussiras

391. *individual/ individuel-individu*

How do you find *individual* cases?	Comment trouves-tu les cas *individuels* ?
It is possible to identify an *individual* vehicle	Il est possible d'identifier un véhicule *individuel*
The *individual* came forward as expected	*L'individu* est arrivé comme atendu

392. *matter/prolème*

This is a *matter* of grave concern.	C'est un *problème* de grande préoccupation
I will go for sure to see the matter	J'irai sûrement voir le *problème*
Don't take the *matter* in your own hands.	Ne prend pas le *problème* en mains

393. *safety/sécurité*

The *safety* is my concern.	La *sécurité* est ma préoccupation
Please watch *safety* of the students.	Fais s'il te plait attention à la *sécurité* des enfants
Safety is a big issue here.	La *sécurtié* est un grand souci ici

394. *turn/tourne-tournure*

Please take a right *turn* here.	*Tourne* s'il te plait à droite ici
Follow the turn of the events.	Suis la *tournure* des évènements
Please *turn* to see the situation	*Tourne* s'il te plait pour vois la situation

395. *everything/tout*

Everything is in perfect order here.	*Tout* est en parfait ordre ici
Try to bring *everything* with you.	Essaie de *tout* ramener avec toi
Everything is fine.	*Tout* est bien

396. *kind/gentil*

He has been very *kind* to me.	Il a été très *gentil* avec moi
He is *kind to everybody*	Il est *gentil* avec tout le monde
I am *kind* to all my students	Je suis *gentil* avec tous mes élèves

397. *quality/qualité*

The *quality* of the food is excellent.	La *qualité* de la nourriture est excellente
Tom does *quality* work.	Tom fait un travail de *qualité*
Do you have better *quality* pictures?	As-tu des photos de meilleure *qualité*

398. *soil/sol*

Nothing seems to grow in this *soil.*	Rien ne semble pousser sur ce *sol*
This *soil* is moist.	Ce *sol* est humide
What will grow in this *soil?*	Que grandira t'il sur ce *sol* ?

399. *ask/demande*

Why do you *ask?*	Que *demandes*-tu ?
May I *ask* a question?	Puis-de *demander* une question ?
Let us *ask* the teacher.	*Demandons* au professeur

400. *board/bord*

Is anyone on *board?*	Y a-t-il quelqu'un au *bord* ?
The ship has everybody on *board*	Ce bateau a tout le monde à *bord*
Is there a doctor on *board?*	Y a-t-il un médecin à *bord* ?

RANKING: 401–500
The most used words

401. Buy Acheter	402. Development Développement	403. Guard Garder	404. Hold Tenir	405. Language Langue
406. Later Après	407. Main Principal	408. Offer Offre	409. Oil Huile	410. Picture Image
411. Potential Potentiel	412. Professional Professionnel	413. Rather Vaut mieux	414. Access Accès	415. Additional Supplémentaire
416. Almost Quasiment	417. Especially Spécialement	418. Garden Jardin	419. International International	420. Lower Inférieur
421. Management Management	422. Open Ouvert	423. Player Joueur	424. Range Eventail	425. Rate Taux
426. Reason Rasion	427. Travel Voyager	428. Variety Variété	429. Video Vidéo	430. Week Demaine
431. Above Dessus	432. According Selon	433. Cook Cuisinier	434. Determine Déterminer	435. Future Avenir
436. Site Site	437. Alternative Alternative	438. Demand Demande	439. Ever Jamais	440. Exercise Exercice
441. Following Suivent	442. Image Image	443. Quickly Vite	444. Special Spécial	445. Working Travaille
446. Case Dossier	447. Cause Cause	448. Coast Côte	449. Probably Probablement	450. Security Sécurité

451. True Vrai	452. Whole Entier	453. Action Action	454. Age Age	455. Among Entre
456. Bad Mauvais	457. Boat Bateau	458. Country Pays/ Campagne	459. Dance Dance	460. Exam Examen
461. Excuse Excuse	462. Grow Grandir- Pousser	463. Movie Film	464. Organization Organisation	465. Record Record
466. Result Résultat	467. Section Section	468. Across A travers	469. Already Déjà	470. Below Dessous
471. Building Bâtiement	472. Mouse Souris	473. Allow Permettre	474. Cash Argent	475. Class Classe
476. Lear Clair	477. Dry Sec	478. Easy Facile	479. Emotional Emotionnel	480. Equipment Equipement
481. Live Vivre	482. Nothing Rien	483. Period Période	484. Physics Pysique	485. Plan Plan
486. Store Boutique	487. Tax Impôt	488. Analysis Analyse	489. Cold Froid	490. Commercial Commercial
491. Directly Directement	492. Full Plein	493. Involved Impliqué	494. Itself Lui-Même	495. Low Bas
496. Old Vieux	497. Policy Politique	498. Political Politique	499. Purchase Acheter	500. Series Séries

401. *buy/acheter*

Do not *buy* these things.	*N'achète* pas ces choses
I am going to *buy* a new handbag.	Je vais *acheter* un nouveau sac à main
What will you *buy* this season?	*Qu'achèteras*-tu cette saison ?

402. *development/développement*

The area needs quick *development.*	Le secteur a besoin d'un *développement* rapide
The project is in the *development* stage.	Le projet est au stade de *développement*
The boy needs more *development.*	Le garçon a besoin de plus de *développement*

403. *guard/garde*

We need a *guard* for the building.	nous avons besoin d'un *gardien* pour l'immeuble
The dogs will *guard* the treasure.	Les chiens *garderont* le trésor
There is no one to *guard* the luggage	Il n'y a personne pour *garder* le bagage

404. *hold/ tenir*

Please *hold* the bag	*Tiens* s'il te plait le sac
This suitcase *holds* everything.	Cette valise *tient* tout
Please *hold* the handrail in the train.	*Tiens* s'il te plait la rampe dans le train

405. *language/langue*

The French is an easy *language* to learn.	Le Français est une *langue* facile à apprendre
The *language* transcends all barriers.	*La langue transcende toutes les barières*
Which *language* is that one?	Quel *langue* est celle-là ?

406. *later/après*

I will see you *later.*	Je te verrai *après*
We will discus this *later.*	On discutera de ça *après*
The meeting has been set for *later*	La réunion a été programmée pour *après*

407. *main/principal*

Please put out the *main* switch	Eteins s'il te plait l'interrupteur *principal*
I will go and check the *main* door.	J'irai vérifier la porte *principal*
Where is the *main* switch?	Où est l'interrupteur *principal* ?

408. *offer/offre-offrir*

This is a very good *offer.*	C'est une très bonne *offre*
How much can you *offer* for this old DVD?	Combien peux-tu *offrir* pour ce vieux DVD ?
I have nothing much to *offer.*	Je n'ai rien à *offrir*

409. *oil/huile*

The Middle East has plenty of olive *oil*	Le moyen orient a beaucoup *d'huile* d'olive
Try to avoid Palm *oil* as much as possible.	Essaie d'éviter *l'huile* de palme
What type of cooking *oil* do you use?	Quel type *d'huile* de cuisine utilises-tu ?

410. *picture/ image*

The *picture* on the wall is really beautiful.	*L'image* sur le mur est très belle
I will buy a *picture* from you.	J'achetrai une *image* de toi
Can you draw a *picture* of me?	Peux –tu peindre une *image* de moi ?

411. *potential/poteniel*

She has the *potential* to do well.	Elle a le *potentiel* de bien faire
Always live up to your *potential.*	Sois toujours à la hauteur de ton *potentiel*
Jim has the *potential* to win a medal.	Jim a le *potentiel* de gagner une médaille

412. *professional/professionnel*

Tim is highly *professional* footballer.	Tim est un Footballer hautement *profesionnel*
You need to be a bit more *professional.*	Tu dois être un peu plus *professionnel*

Are you not a *professional* wrestler?	N'es-tu pas un lutteur *professionnel* ?

413. *rather/vaut mieux*

Rather you could work	Il *vaut mieux* que tu puisses travailler
I would *rather* not go	Il *vaut mieux* que je n'aille pas
I should *rather* stay at home	Il *vaut mieux* que je reste à la maison

414. *access/accès*

I do not have *access* to any of these vaults.	Je n'ai *accès* à aucun des ces coffres
Do you have an *access* card?	As-tu une cate *d'accès* ?
Why am I not allowed *access* these files?	Pourquoi n'ai-je pas *accès* à ces fichiers ?

415. *additional/supplémentaire*

You need to write some *additional* notes.	Tu dois ecrire quelques notes *supplémentaires*
We need *additional* help	Nous avons besoin d'aide *suppélementaire*
This book has some *additional* information.	Ce livre a quelque information *suppélmentaire*

416. *almost/quasiment*

She is *almost* there.	Elle est *quasiment* là-bas

I have *almost* finished this thesis.	*J'ai quasiment fini cette thèse*
I am *almost* certain that Jim is the murderer.	Je suis *quasiment* sûr que Jim est l'assassin

417. *especially/spécialement*

I love everybody in office *especially* you.	J'aime tout le monde au bureau *spécialement* toi
I miss her, *especially* on rainy days.	Ele me manque, *spécialement* dans les jours pluvieux
She is always *especially* nice	Elle est toujours *spécialement* gentille

418. *garden/jardin*

The *garden* needs to be manicured.	Le *jardin* doit être entretenu
There is no one to look after the *garden.*	Il n'y a personne pour s'occuper du *jardin*
You have a beautiful *garden* on the terrace.	Tu as un beau *jardin* à la térasse

419. *international/international*

The *international* laws are valid here	Les lois *internationales* sont valides ici
Do not enter the *international* airspace	N'entre pas dans l'espace aérien *international*
The *international* committee will investigate	Le comité *international* investiguera

420. *lower/ inférieur*

She has a sore spot in her *lower* back.	Elle a un pont douloureux dans son dos *inférieur*
She bit her *lower* lip.	Elle a mordu sa lèvre *inférieure*
I got the *lower* berth in train.	J'ai eu la couchette *inférieur* en train

421. *management/ management*

The *management* stood by its decision.	Le *management* se tient à sa décision
The *management* has specific views.	Le *management* a des opinions spécifiques
She went to Scotland to study *management.*	Elle est partie en Ecosse pour étudier le *management*

422. *open/ouvert*

The door was left *open.*	La porte a été laissée *ouverte*
Open the door for your teacher.	*Ouvre* la porte pour ton professeur
I kept the fridge door *open* by mistake.	J'ai gardé la *porte* du refrégirateur *ouverte* par erreur

423. *player/joueur*

He is the most talented *player* in our team.	Il est le *joueur* le plus talentueux dans notre équipe
The *player* was hurt in the match.	Le *joueur* a été blessé dans le match
Do you have any news about the	As-tu des informations sur le *joueur* ?

player?	

424. *range/Eventail*

There is a wide *range* of reasons	Il ya un grand *éventail* de raisons
My skills show a wide *range.*	Mes compétences montrent un large *éventail*
The store has a good *range* of products.	La boutique a un large *éventail* de produits

425. *rate/taux*

What is the exchange *rate* today?	Quel est le *taux* de change aujourd'hui ?
That is the going *rate.*	C'est le *taux* courant
At any *rate* I will do my best.	A n'importe quel *taux* je ferai de mon mieux

426. *reason/raison*

What is the *reason* for her absence?	Quelle est la *raison* de son absence ?
You need to find the *reason* behind it.	Tu dois trouver la *raison* derrière ça
I don't see the *reason* to do that	Je ne vois pas la *raison* de faire ça

427. *travel/voyager*

I like to *travel* a lot.	J'aime *voyager* beaucoup

Do you love to *travel?*	Aimes-tu *voyager* ?
I have to *travel* a lot in my work.	Je dois *voyager* beaucoup ans mon travail

428. *variety/variété*

There is a wide *variety* of goods	Il y a une large *variété* de biens
There is no *variety* in the restaurant menu.	Il n'y a pas de *variété* dans le menu du restaurant
Look at the *variety* of flowers.	Regarde la *variété* des fleurs

429. *video/vidéo*

The *video* was very disturbing.	La *vidéo* était troublante
The security guard checked the *video*	L'agent de sécurité a vérifié la *vidéo*
Did you watch any online *video?*	Regardes-tu des *vidéos* en ligne ?

430. *week/semaine*

Please come here next *week.*	S'il te plait viens ici la *semaine* prochaine
I am very busy this *week.*	Je suis occupé cette *semaine*
What a *week* that was!	Quelle *semaine* ça était !

431. *above/au-dessus*

He lives *above* me.	Il habite au-*dessus* de moi

He is *above* doing such a thing.	Il est au-*dessus* de faire une telle chose
Tom lives in the room *above* us.	Tom habite dans la chambre au-*dessus* de nous

432. *according/selon*

According to Tom, Jill is not coming today.	*Selon* Tom, Jill ne viendra pas aujourd'hui
You should work *according* to a set plan.	Tu dois travail *selon* un plan défini
According to you, what should be next?	*Selon* toi, que devrait suivre ?

433. *cook/cuisinier*

We have an Italian *cook* at home.	Nous avons un *cuisinier* italien à la maison
The *cook* in our house is gone	Le *cuisinier* dans notre maison est parti
Tom is a good *cook*.	Tom est un bon *cuisinier*

434. *détermine/détérminer*

I will *determine* how we proceed.	Je *déterminerai* comment procéder
We couldn´t *determine* her whereabouts.	Nous ne pouvions pas *déterminer* son sort
We are trying to *determine* what happened	Nous essayons de *déterminer* ce qui s'est passé

435. *future/avenir*

The *future* looks good for Tom.	*L'avenir* semble bien pour Tom
I can foresee my *future.*	Je peux *prévoir* l'avenir
Do not rely on *future* predictions.	Ne te fie pas aux prédictions *d'avenir*

436. *site/site*

Bookmark this *site.*	Marque ce *site*
This *site* is quite useful.	Ce *site* est très utile
A man appeared at the *site.*	Un homme est apparu au *site*

437. *alternative/alternative*

There seems to be no *alternative*	Il semble y avoir une *alternative*
Is there an *alternative* room?	Y a-t-il une chambre *alternative* ?
Do you have an *alternative* plan?	As-tu un plan *alternatif* ?

438. *demand/demande*

I *demand* a salary hike immediately	Je *demande* une augmentation de salaire immédiatement
Is there any *demand* for this product/	Y a-t-il une *demande* pour ce produit ?
Your *demand* cannot be met.	Votre *demande* ne peut pas être satisfaite

439. *ever/jamais*

Have you *ever* been on TV?	es-tu *jamais* passé à la télé ?

Have you *ever* been mugged?	As-tu *jamais* été agressé ?
Have you *ever* seen a whale?	As-tu *jamais* vu une baleine ?

440. *exercise/exercice*

Regular *exercise* is good for the body.	*L'exercice* régulier est bon pour le corps
Early *exercises* are healthy	Les *exercices* matinaux sont bon pour la santé
Do you *exercise* regularly?	*Exerces*-tu régulièrement ?

441. *following/suivent/suis*

A lof of people is *following* Obama	Beaucoup de gens *suivent* Obama
I am *following* him for a long time.	Je le *suis* depuis longtemps
Are you *following* what he is saying?	*Suis*-tu ce qu'il dit ?

442. *image/image*

The *image* of the club is very good.	*L'image* du club est très bonne
These are really rare *images.*	Ce sont vraiment de rares *images*
Where did you get this *image?*	Où as-tu eu cette *image* ?

443. quickly/vite

Come here *quickly.*	Viens ici *vite*
I *quickly* ate lunch.	J'ai *vite* mangé le déjeuner

Fashions change *quickly.*	Les modes changent *vite*

444. *special/especial*

He has got *special* talents.	Il a eu des talents *spéciaux*
He is really very *special* to me.	Il est vraiement très *spécial* pour moi
I will cook something *special* for you.	Je cuisinerai quelque chose *spéciale* pour toi

445. *working/travaille*

I am *working* in a multi-national firm.	Je *travaille* dans une société multinationale
How long have you been *working?*	Depuis combien de temps *travailles-* tu ?
She is *working* in this hospital	Elle *travaille* dans l'hôpital

446. *case/dossier*

This is a very hard *case* to crack.	C'est un *dossier* très difficile à résoudre
I will defend my *case* .	Je défendrai mon *dossier*
This *case* is irrelevant	Ce *dossier* est hors sujet

447. *cause/cause*

What has been the *cause* of this fire?	Quelle a été la *cause* de ce feu ?
Do not *cause* any further trouble,	Ne *cause* pas plus de problème s'il te

please.	plait
Dandruff is the *cause* of your problems.	Dandruff est la *casue* de tes problèmes

448. *coast/côte*

Tom went to college on the West *coast.*	Tom est parti au collège à la *côte* Ouest
The *coast* is clear.	La *côte* est claire
I am from the East *coast.*	Je suis de la *côte E*st

449. *probably/probablement*

He is *probably* sleeping.	Il dort *probablement*
Dinner is *probably* ready	Le diner est *probablement* prêt
We *probably* won't have much snow	On aura *probalement* pas beaucoup de neige

450. *security/sécurité*

The *security* guard is the suspect.	L'agent de sécurité est le *suspect*
I will look after her *security.*	Je m'occuperai de la *sécurité*
There is no *security* for women	Il n'y a pas de *sécurité* pour les femmes

451. *true/vrai*

Is that *true?*	Est-ce *vrai* ?
Dreams come *true.*	Les rêves deviennent *vrais*

This story is *true.*	Cette histoire est *vraie*

452. *whole/entier*

I will eat the *whole* cake today	Je mangerai le gâteau *entier* aujourd'hui
The *whole* world is going mad	Le monde *entier* devient fou
My *whole* body is sore	Mon corps *entier* est douloureux

453. *action/action*

Western leaders condemned the *action*	les leaders d'ouest on condamné *l'action*
Action is more important than words.	*L'action* est plus importante que les mots
His brave *action* is worthy of a medal.	Son *action* courageuse mérite une médaille

454. *age/âge*

I am the same *age.*	J'ai le même *âge*
He is about my *age.*	Il est de mon *âge*
I am twice your *age.*	Je fais deux fois ton *âge*

455. *among/entre*

We agreed *among* ourselves.	Nous avons convenu *entre* nous

Tom uneasy *among* strangers.	Tom est inquiet *entre* les étrangers
He believes there is a spy *among* us.	Il croit qu'il ya un espion *entre* nous

456. *bad/mauvais*

The food was really *bad.*	La nourriture était vraiment *mauvaise*
His behavior is very *bad.*	Son comportement est très *mauvais*
Jim has a *bad* attitude towards his sister.	Jim a une *mauvaise* attitude envers sa sœur

457. *boat/ bateau*

They got into the *boat.*	Il sont montés dans le *bateau*
You can go there in a *boat.*	Tu peux aller là-bas en *bateau*
I crossed the river by *boat.*	J'ai traversé la rivère en *bateau*

458. *country/pays-campagne*

I live in the *country.*	Je vis à la *campagne*
My parents live in the *country.*	Mes parents vivent à la *campagne*
Switzerland is a neutral *country.*	La Suisse est un *pays* neutre

459. *dance/dance*

Jim loved to watch tribal *dance.*	Jim aime regarder la *dance* tribale
Mary can *dance* well.	Mary peut bien *dancer*

She watched him *dance.*	Elle l'a regardé *dancer*

460. *exam/examen*

I have a history *exam* tomorrow.	J'ai un *examen* d'histoire demain
You need an eye *exam.*	Tu as besoin d'un *examen* de l'œil
Did you submit your *exam* papers?	As-tu rendu ta feuille *d'examen* ?

461. *excuse/ excuse*

Excuse my clumsiness	*Excuse* ma maladresse
Excuse me, but I feel sick	*Excuse*-moi mais je me sens malade
Excuse me for opening your letter	*Excuse* moi d'avoir ouvert ta lettre

462. *grow/pousse -grandir*

Here *grows wheat*	Ici *pousse* le blé
Nothing seems to *grow* in this soil.	Rien ne semble *pousser* sur ce sol
What do you want to be when you *grow* up?	Que veux-tu devenir quand tu *grandiras* ?

463. *movie/film*

Was the *movie* good?	Le *film* est bien ?
Let us go to a *movie.*	Allons voir un *film*
Did you like the *movie?*	As-tu aimé le *film* ?

464. *organization/organisation*

UN is a highly respected *organization.*	L'ONU est une *organisation* très respectée
I will join a new *organization.*	Je joindrai une nouvelle *organisation*
The *organization* began its activities.	*L'organisation* a commencé ces activités

465. *record/ record/rappel*

Jack set a new world *record*	Jack a établi un nouveau *record* mondial
Her *record* in this event is deplorable.	Son *record* dans ce nouvel évènement est deplorable
Did you say anything for the *record*?	As-tu dis quelque chose pour *rappel* ?

466. *result/résultat*

Tom wants *results.*	Tom veux des *résultats*
These are the *results.*	Voici les *résultats*
We expect good *results.*	Nous attendond de bons *résultats*

467. *section/section*

I look after the licensing *section*	Je m'occupe de la *section* d'accréditation
Here, the poorer *section* of the society	Ici, la *section* la plus pauvre de la société

This *section* is for food storage	Cette *section* est pour le stockege de la nourriture

468. *across/à travers*

He can walk *across* the street.	Il peut marcher à *travers* le boulevard
I can swim *across* the river.	Je peux nager à *travers* la rivière
We flew *across* the Atlantic.	Nous avons volé à *travers* l'atlantique

469. *already/déjà*

He has *already* left.	Il a *déjà* quitté
He had *already* gone.	Il est *déjà* parti
Has he arrived *already*?	Il est arrivée *déjà* ?

470. *below/dessous*

It is five degrees *below* normal	Il fait 5 degrés au-*dessous* de la normale
The neighbor below is noisy	Le voisin de *dessous* est bruyant
The flat *below* has a nice view	L'appartement de *dessous* a une jolie vue

471. *building/bâtiment*

What is that *building*?	C'est quoi ce *bâtiement* ?
Look at that *building*.	Regarde ce *bâtiment*

What is that tall *building*?	C'est quoi ce grand *bâtiment* ?

472. *mouse/souris*

I saw a *mouse* today.	J'ai vu une *souris* aujourd'hui
It was a large *mouse*.	C'était une grande *souris*
I need a new *mouse* for the PC	J'ai besoin d'une nouvelle *souris* pour l'ordinateur

473. *allow/permettre*

I cannot *allow* him here.	Je ne peux pas le *permettre* ici
Please *allow* me to write the final answer.	*Permettez*-moi s'il vous plait d'écrire la dernière réponse
The teacher will never *allow* all this	Le professeur ne *permettra* jamais ça

474. *cash/argent*

I need lots of *cash* today.	J'ai besoin de beaucoup *d'argent* aujourd'hui
Please pay the *cash* to Jim	Payez s'il vous plait *l'argent* à Jim
A lot of *cash* is available	Beaucoup *d'argent* est disponible

475. *class/classe*

Jill got promoted to higher *class*	Jill a été promu à une *classe* supérieure
There is a *class* division in the society.	Il y une division de *classe* dans la

	société
The seats in the 2nd *class* are not nice	Les sièges dans la 2ème *classe* ne sont pas jolis

476. *clear/clair*

The sky is *clear.*	Le ciel est *clair*
Do I make myself *clear*?	Suis-je *clair* ?
Am I making myself *clear*?	Suis-je *clair* ?

477. *dry/sec-sèche*

Paul has *dry* hair.	Paul a des cheuveux *secs*
I only buy *dry* food for the fishes.	J'achète seulement de la nourriture *sèche* pour les poissons
My dog never eats *dry* food.	Mon chien ne mange jamais de la nourriture *sèche*

478.*easy/facile-facilement*

Paul is an *easy* going person.	Paul est une personne *facile* à vivre
The SAT papers were real *easy.*	Les papiers de SAT étaient réellement *facile*
I never had it so *easy.*	Je ne l'ai jamais eu au *facilement*

479. *emotional/émotionnel*

Paul is a very *emotional* person.	Paul est une personne très *émotionnelle*
This is the most *emotional* book I have read	C'est le livre le plus *émotionnel* que j'ai lu
Why are you being so *emotional*?	Pourquoi es-tu si *émotionnel* ?

480. *equipment /équipement*

What photographic *equipment* do you use?	Quel *équipement* photographique utilises-tu ?
His *equipment* was seized at the airport.	Son *équipement* était saisi à l'aéroport
This *equipment* is the best available	Cet *équipement* et le meilleur disponible

481. *live* /vis-vécu

I *live* in Japan.	Je *vis* au Japon
Did you *live* here?	As-tu *vécu* ici ?
I *live* in the country.	Je *vis* à la campagne

482 *nothing/rien*

There is *nothing* in the attic.	Il n'y a *rien* dans le grenier
Nothing is left of the chocolate cake.	*Rien* ne reste du gâteau de chocolat
Nothing can stop us now.	*Rien* ne peut nous arrêter maintenant

483. Period/période

It is the most important *period* in my life.	C'est la *périonde* la plus importante de ma vie
This is a *period* of mourning.	C'est une *période* de deuil
This *period* of uncertainty will be over.	Cette *période* d'incertitude sera finie

484. Physics/physique

Physics is my favorite subject.	La *physique* est mon sujet favori
I got a B+ in *Physics*.	J'ai eu un B+ en *physique*
The *Physics* teacher was late	Le profésseur de *physique* était en retard

485. Plan/plan

There was no *plan* for the team	Il n'y avait pas de *plan* pour l'équipe
Do you have a *plan* for tomorrow?	As-tu un *plan* pour demain ?
I have an amazing *plan*.	J'ai un *plan* génial

486. Store/boutique

She took him to the *store*.	Elle l'a emmené à la *boutique*
What did she buy at the *store*?	Qu'a t'elle acheté à la *boutique*?
I met Jack in front of the *store*.	J'ai rencontré Jack devant la *boutique*

487. Tax/impôt

You must pay your *tax* on time.	Tu dois payer ton *impôt* à temps
Every person must pay taxes.	Tout le monde doit payer les *impôts*
Where can I pay the toll *tax*?	Où puis-je payer *l'impôt* ?

488. Analysis/analyse

The final *analysis* is ready	*L'analyse* final est prête
Make an *analysis* of the balance sheets	Fais une *analyse* du bilan
The *analysis* of stock values is boring	*L'analyse* est valeurs des actions est ennuyeuse

489. Cold/froid

It was very *cold* outside.	Il faisiat très *froid* dehors
The polar bear lives in *cold* temperatures.	L'ours polaire vit dans une température *froide*
The cold *food was* delicious.	La nourriture *froide* était délicieuse

490. Commercial/commercial

Did you pay the *commercial* taxes?	As-tu payé la taxe *commerciale* ?
The car is not for *commercial* purposes.	la voiture n'est pas pour des fins *commerciales*
You need to have a *commercial* permit.	Tu dois avoir un permis *commercial*

491. *directly/directment*

He was directly involved in the robbery	Il était *directement* impliqué dans le vol
I was never *directly* involved	Je n'ai jamais été *directement* impliqué
Please speak to him *directly*	Parle lui *directement* s'il te plait

492. *full/plein-totale*

My stomach is *full.*	Mon estomac est *plein*
The car has a *full* tank.	Le réservoir de la voiture est *plein*
I am waiting for the *full* disclosure	J'attends la révélation *totale*

493. *involved/impliqué*

I don't want to get *involved* in all these.	Je ne veux pas être *impliqué* dans tout ça
She was never *involved* in the plan.	Elle n'a jamais été *impliqué* dans le plan
I was *involved* in my work	J'étais *impliqué* dans mon travail

494. *itself/elle-même – lui-même*

The chair adjusts *itself.*	La chaise s'ajuste *d'elle-même*
Life *itself* is an effective therapist.	La vie *elle-même* est un thérapeute efficace
The snake curled *itself* around her body.	Le serpent s'entroule *lui-même* autour de son corps

495. *low/bas*

Keep the flame *low.*	Garde la flamme *basse*
The chair is too *low* for me	La chaise est trop *basse* pour moi
She complained about her *low* salary	Elle s'est plainte de son *bas* salaire

496. *old/vieux-vielle-âge*

I am *old* enough for this.	Je suis assez *vieux* pour ça
My mother has grown very *old.*	Ma mère est devenue très *vielle*
How *old* are you?	Quel *âge* as-tu ?

497. *policy/politique*

The government announced its new *policy.*	Le gouvernement a annoncé sa nouvelle *politique*
The reason for the new *policy* is unknown	La raison de la nouvelle *politique* est inconnue
The inmigration *policy* is very restricting	La *politique* d'immigration est très restrictive

498. *political/politique*

The environment is very *political.*	L'ambiance est très *politique*
Do not get involved in *political* activities.	Ne sois pas impliqué dans des activités *politiques*
Have you joined any *political* party?	As-tu rejoins un parti *politique* ?

499. *purchase/acheter*

Did Tom *purchase* it?	Est-ce que Tom l'a *acheté* ?
When did you *purchase* it?	Quand l'as-tu *acheté* ?
I borrowed money to *purchase* the car.	J'ai emprunter de l'argent pour *acheter* la voiture

500. *series/serie*

The soccer *series* ended in a draw.	Les *séries* du football se sont terminées en nul
They played a three match *series*	Il ont joué des *séries* de trois matchs
Ferrari opted for this high profile *series.*	Ferrari a opté pour les *séries* de haut profile

RANKING: 501-600
The most used words

501. Side Côté	502. Subject Sujet	503. Supply Fournir	504. Therefore Donc	505. Thought Pensais
506. Basis Base	507. Boyfriend Petit Ami	508. Deal Gérer/Accord	509. Direction Direction	510. Mean Signifier
511. Primary Primaire	512. Space Espace	513. Strategy Stratégie	514. Technology Technologie	515. Worth Mérite
516. Army Armée	517. Camera Caméra	518. Fall Tomber Automne	519. Freedom Liberté	520. Paper Papier
521. Rule Règle	522. Similar Similaire	523. Stock Stock	524. Weather Climat	525. Yet Déjà
526. Bring Apporter	527. Chance Chance	528. Environment Environnement	529. Everyone Tout le monde	530. Figure Visage
531. Improve Améliorer	532. Man Homme	533. Model Mannequin	534. Necessary Nécessaire	535. Positive Positif
536. Produce Produire	537. Search Recherche	538. Source Source	539. Beginning Début	540. Child Enfant
541. Earth Terre	542. Else Autre	543. Health Santé	544. Instance Exemple	545. Maintain Maintenir
546. Month	547. Present	548. Program	549. Spend	550. Talk

Mois	Présent	Programme	Passer/ Dépenser	Parler
551. Truth Vérité	552. Upset Furieux	553. Begin Commencer	554. Chicken Poulet	555. Close Fermer
556. Creative Créatif	557. Design Design	558. Feature Caractéristique	559. Financial Financier	560. Head Directeur/Chef
561. Marketing Marketing	562. Material Matériel	563. Medical Médical	564. Purpose But/Raison	565. Question Question
566. Rock Rock/Rocher	567. Salt Sel	568. Tell Dire	569. Themselves Se Eux-même	570. Traditional Traditionnel
571. University Université	572. Writing Ecriture	573. Act Agir	574. Article Article	575. Birth Naissance
576. Car Voiture	577. Cost Coût	578. Department Département	579. Difference Différence	580. Dog Chien
581. Drive Conduire	582. Exist Existe	583. Federal Fédéral	584. Goal But	585. Green Vert
586. Late Tard/Retard	587. News Infos	588. Object Objet	589. Scale Echelle Balance	590. Sun Soleil
591. Support Support	592. Tend Tendre	593. Thus Ainsi	594. Audience Audience	595. Enjoy Apprécie
596. Entire Entier	597. Fishing Pêche	598. Fit Rentre	599. Glad Heureux	600. Growth Croissance

501. *side/côté*

The player has a serious injury on his *side*	Le joueur a une blessure sérieuse sur son *côté*
Come over to this *side*.	Viens de ce *côté*
Walk on the left *side* of the road.	Marche du *côté* de gauche de la route

502. *subject/sujet*

What is your favorite *subject* in school?	Quel est ton *sujet* préféré à l'école ?
History was never the *subject* I liked.	L'histoire n'a jamais été le *sujet* que j'aime
The man has an opinion on this theme.	L'homme a une option sur ce *sujet*

503. *supply/fourniture-fournis*

The gas *supply* to building was cut off.	La *fourniture* du gaz au batiment a été interrompue
There ia a steady *supply* of fresh milk.	Il y a une *fourniture* régilère du lait frais
Please *supply* chicken on a regular basis?	*Fournis* s'il te plait le poulet à de façon régulière

504. *therefore/donc*

Therefore they should be better now.	*Donc* ils doivent être meiux maintenant

I was a skeptical; *therefore* I avoided him.	J'étais sceptique ; *Donc* je l'ai évité
It is very early, *therefore* you should wait	C'est très tôt. *Donc* tu dois attendre

505. *thought/pensait*

Jim *thought* that it was a bad joke.	Jim *pensait* que c'était une mauvaise blague
I never *thought* on those lines.	Je n'ai jamais *pensé* de cette manière
Give a *thought* to the lyrics of the song.	Donne une *pensée* aux paroles de la chanson

506. *basis/base*

On what *basis* did you take this decision?	Sur quelle *base* as-tu pris cette décision
There is no *basis* for these claims.	Il n'y a pas de *base* pour cette reclamation
That is my *basis* for saying so.	C'est ma *base* pour dire ainsi

507. *boyfriend/petit ami*

Her *boyfriend* looks younger than her.	Son *petit ami* semble plus jeune qu'elle
Look at her *boyfriend*!	Regarde son *petit ami*
Her *boyfriend* is very handsome.	Son *petit ami* est très beau

508. *deal/gérer-accord*

Let us *deal* with the problem	Essayons de *gérer* le problème
I have a lot to deal with	Je dois beaucoup *gérer*
A *deal* is a *deal*	Un *accord* est un *accord*

509. *direction/direction*

Can you please give the proper *direction*?	Peux-tu s'il te plait me donner la bonne *direction* ?
Your career is in the right *direction.*	Ta carrière est dans la bonne *direction*
The man goes in the wrong *direction*	L'homme est allé dans la mauvaise *direction*

510. *mean/ voulais dire-signifie*

I don't *mean* that	Je ne *voulais* pas *dire* ça
What does it *mean*?	Que *signifie* t'il ?
What I *mean* is this.	Ce que je *voulais dire* c'est ça

511. *primary/primaire*

The *primary* goal is to win the match.	L'objectif *primaire* est de gagner le match
The kid was admitted in the *primary* school.	L'enfant a été admis à l'école *primaire*
I need the *primary* school textbooks	J'ai besoin des livres de l'école *primaire*

512. *space/espace*

Traveling to *space* was his childhood dream	Voyager à *l'espace* était son rêve d'enfant
She was the first woman in *space.*	Elle était la première femme dans *l'espace*
Laika was the first dog in *space.*	Laika était la première chienne dans *l'espace*

513. *strategy/stratégie*

What is your *strategy* for this match?	Quelle est ta *stratégie* pour ce match ?
He has a *strategy* to defend the bridge.	Il a une *stratégie* pour défendre le pont
He decided to adopt a defensive *strategy*	Il a décidé d'adopter une *stratégie* défensive

514. *technology/technologie*

The developed countries have *technology*	Les pays développés ont la *technologie*
Technology made life simpler.	La *technologie* rend la vie plus simple
This is the latest *technology* for agriculture	C'est la dernière *technologie* pour l'agriculture

515. *worth/mérite*

The watch is definitely not *worth* the price	La montre ne *mérite* absolument pas le prix
I think it is *worth* a try.	Je pense que ça *mérite* un essai

New York is *worth* visiting.	New York *mérite* une viste

516. *army/armée*

The US *Army* is well equipped	*L'armée* des Etats-Unis est bie néquipée
They used the *army* to restore peace	Il ont utilisé *l'armée* pour instaurer la paix
If you join the *army* you serve the nation.	Si tu rejoins *l'armée* tu serviras la nation

517. *camera/caméra*

I need to buy a digital *camera*	Je dois acheter une *caméra* numérique
The *camera* fell from his hand and broke	La *caméra* est tombée de sa main et s'est cassée
Jack bought a new Nikon *camera.*	Jack a acheté une nouvelle *caméra* Nikon

518. *fall/ tombée-automne*

She was injured in the *fall.*	Elle s'est blessée dans la *tombée*
We moved to New York last *fall.*	Nous sommes allées à New York l' *automne* dernier
Leaves begin to *fall* in October.	Les feuilles commencent à *tomber* en Octobre

519. *freedom/liberté*

The nation gained *freedom* in1945	La nation a gagné la *liberté* en 1945
The prisoner was given his *freedom.*	Le prisionier a été donné la *liberté*
The man yearned for *freedom*	L'homme a aspiré à la *liberté*

520. *paper/papier*

I need some *paper.*	J'ai besoin du *papier*
I want some *paper.*	Je veux du *papier*
Paper burns easily.	Le *papier* brule facilement

521. *rule/règle*

You broke the *rule.*	Tu as enfreins la *règle*
This *rule* has no exceptions.	Cette *règle* n'a pas d'exceptions
Will you explain the *rule* to me?	Peux tu m'expliquer la *règle* ?

522. *similar/similaire*

We are very *similar.*	Nous sommes très *similaires*
Your problem is *similar* to mine.	Ton problème est *similaire* au mien
I saw a *similar* painting somewhere else.	J'ai vu une peinture *similaire* ailleurs

523. *stock/stock*

We run out of *stock*	Nous sommes à court de *stock*

We are out of *stock*.	Nous sommes à cours de *stock*
What made you buy that *stock*?	Qu'est ce qui t'as fait acheter ce *stock* ?

524. *weather/climat*

The *weather* looks fine today.	Le *climat* semble joli aujourd'hui
The *weather* stayed bad.	Le *climat* est resté mauvais
I am sick of this hot *weather*.	Je suis malade de ce *climat* chaud

525. *yet/déjà*

Has he come *yet*?	Est-t'il *déjà* arrivée ?
I am ready *yet*.	Je suis *déjà* prêt
Have you fed the dog *yet*?	As-tu *déjà* nourri le chien ?

526. *bring/apporter*

Please *bring* the books with you.	*Apporte* s'il te plait le livre avec toi
Tom should *bring* the pen he took yesterday.	Tom doit *apporter* le stylo qu'il a pris hier
I will *bring* the food, don't worry.	*J'apporterai* la nourriture. Ne t'inquiète pas

527. *chance/chance*

He has a genuine *chance* of qualification.	Il a une *chance* de se qualifier

There is a chance to met him	Il y a une *chance* de le rencontrer
There is still a *chance.*	Il y a encore une *chance*

528. *environment/environnement*

We must protect the *environment.*	Nous devons protéger *l'environnement*
We live in the *environment*	Nous vivons dans *l'environnement*
This is bad for the *environment.*	C'est mauvais pour *l'environnement*

529. *everyone/tout le monde*

Everyone likes her	*Tout le monde* l'apprécie
Everyone loves him	*Tout le monde* l'aime
He is known to *everyone*	Il est connu de *tout le monde*

530. *figure/visage-personnages*

That girl had had a nice *figure.*	Cette fille a un joli *visage*
They were *figures* in a landscape.	Il y avait des *personnages* le paysage
Jill has a very attractive *figure.*	Jill a un *visage* très attractif

531. *improve/améliorer*

You need to *improve* your handwriting.	Tu dois *améliorer* ton écriture
Maybe his mood will *improve* today.	Peut être son humeur *s'améliorera* aujourd'hui
These medicines will *improve* his	Ces médicaments vont *améliorer* sa

condition.	condition

532. *man/homme*

The *man* looks very angry.	*L'homme* semble très en colère
Look at that *man*!	Regarde cet *homme*
The *man* slowly walked towards outside	*L'homme* a marché lentement vers l'extérieur

533. *model/mannequin*

He is a famous *model.*	Il est un *mannequin* célèbre
Are you a *mode*l ?	Es-tu un *mannequin* ?
Mary is a renowned *model.*	Mary est une *mannequin* réputée

534. *necessary/nécessaire*

I will come if *necessary.*	Je viendrai si *nécessaire*
It is *necessary* for you to go.	C'est *nécessaire* pour toi d'aller
It has been *necessary* to get a loan.	Il était *nécessaire* de prendre un prêt

535. *positive/positif*

The players sounded very *positive*	Les joueurs doivent être très *positifs*
You should always have a *positive* attitude	Tu dois toujours avoir une attitude *positive*
Always be *positive* before an exam.	Sois toujours *positif* avec l'examen

536. *produce/produit*

England imports Spanish *produce.*	L'Angleterre importe des *produits* espagnols
These fields *produce* fine crops.	Ces terrains *produisent* de bonnes cultures
We cannot *produce* without raw materials	Nous ne pouvons pas *produire* sans matière première

537. *search/recherche*

The police initiated *search* operations	La police a inité l'opération de *recherche*
Our *search* did not last long.	Notre *recherche* n'a pas duré longtemps
A *search* of the building needs to be done	Une *recherche* du batiment doit être faite

538. *source/source*

What is the *source* of your information?	Quelles est la *source* de votre information
Never reveal your *source* to anybody.	Ne révèle ta *source* à personne
The river flows freely from its *source*	La rivières coule librement de sa *source*

539. *beginning/début*

I missed the *beginning* of the film.	J'ai manqué le *début* du film
The *beginning* of the book is a bit boring.	Le *début* du livre est un peu ennuyeux
The *beginning* of the film is awesome	Le *début* du film est génial

540. *child/enfant*

We adopted a *child.*	Nous avons adopté un *enfant*
Are you the only *child*?	Es-tu le seul *enfant* ?
I am no longer a *child.*	Je ne suis plus un *enfant*

541. *earth/terre*

The *earth* is round.	La *terre* est ronde
He is the richest man on *earth.*	Il est l'homme le plus riche sur *terre*
I am the happiest man on *earth.*	Je suis l'homme le plus heureux sur *terre*

542. *else/d'autre*

Please ask someone *else.*	Demande s'il te plait quelq'un *d'autre*
There is not anybody *else.*	Il n'y a personne *d'autre*
Who *else* came to the party?	Qui *d'autre* est venu à la fête ?

543. *healthy/sain*

I am *healthy*.	Je suis *sain*
He looks *healthy*.	Il semble *sain*
I had a *healthy* breakfast.	J'ai eu un petit-déjeuner *sain*

544. *instance/exemple*

There has been no such *instance* in the past.	Il n'a pas eu un tel *exemple* dans le passé
For *instance*, he hit many people	*Par exemple*, il a frappé plusieurs gens
For *instance*, I don't think it was a mistake	*Par exemple*, je ne pense pas que c'était une erreur

545. *maintain/maintenir*

We should make efforts to *maintain* peace	Nous devons faire des efforts pour *maintenir* la paix
I *maintain* that I am not to blame	Je *maintiens* que je ne suis pas à blâmer
He is trying to *maintain* 2 jobs.	Il essaie de *maintenir* 2 travaux

546. *month/mois*

I moved last *month*.	J'ai déménagé le *mois* dernier
I will see you next *month*.	Je te verrai le *mois* prochain
We are moving next *month*.	Nous déménagerons le *mois* prochain

547. *present/present*

He accepted my *present.*	Il a accepté mon *présent*
She gave him a *present.*	Elle lui a donné un *présent*
Forty people were *present.*	Quanrante personnes étaient *présentes*

548. *program/programme*

He developed a software *program*	Il a développé un *programme* logiciel
The schedule of the *program* was released	L'horaire du *programme* était sorti
The *program* is already on the air	Le *programme* est déjà diffusé

549. *spend/passer-dépenser*

How did you *spend* your vacation?	Comment as-tu *passé* tes vacances ?
Do you *spend* much time writing?	*Passes*-tu beaucoup de temps en lisant
How much money did you *spend*?	Combien d'argent as-tu *dépensé* ?

550. *talk/parler*

They stopped to *talk.*	Ils ont arrêté de *parler*
Can we *talk* in private?	Pouvons-nous *parler* en privé ?
Do you *talk* to your dog?	*Parles*-tu à ton chien ?

551. *truth/vérité*

Tell me the *truth.*	Dis-moi la *vérité*
Did he tell you the *truth*?	T'a-t-il dit la *vérité* ?
That is the absolute *truth.*	C'est la *vérité* absolue

552. *upset/furieux-troublé*

I was *upset* after the results.	J'étais *furieux* après les résultats
I am afraid I have an *upset* stomach.	J'ai peur d'avoir un estomac *troublé*
Tom looks very *upset.*	Tom semble très *furieux*

553. *begin/commencer*

Let us *begin.*	*Commençons*
When does it *begin*?	Quand *commence*-t'il
Let us *begin* on page 30.	*Commençons* à la page 30

554. *chicken/poulet*

She bought *chicken.*	Elle a acheté le *poulet*
I do not eat *chicken* skin.	Je ne mange pas la peau du *poulet*
I saw the man feed his chicken	J'ai vu l'homme nourrir ses *poulets*

555. *close/fermer*

Close your book.	*Ferme* ton livre
Close your eyes.	*Ferme* tes yeux

Please *close* the door.	*Ferme* s'il te plait la porte

556. *creative/créatif*

Jim is very *creative.*	Jim est très *créatif*
You need to have a *creative* mind	Tu dois avoir un esprit *créatif*
This work of art looks very *creative.*	Ce travail d'art semble très *créatif*

557. *design/design*

The *design* of the building is almost flawless.	Le *design* du batiment est presque parfait
Tom does not like the *design* at all.	Tom n'aime pas le *design* du tout
I am studying web *design.*	J'étudie le *design* web

558. *feature/caractéristique*

The most important *feature* is this.	La *caractéristique* la plus importante est celle-là
Google introduced a new *feature*	Google a introduit une nouvellle *caractéristique*
What is the main *feature*?	Quelle est la *caractéristique* principale ?

559. *financial/financier*

I need *financial* advice.	J'ai besoin de conseil *financier*

Tom is facing *financial* problems.	Tom fait face à des problèmes *financiers*
Tom needs *financial* help.	Tom a besoin d'une aide *financière*

560. *head/directeur-chef*

The *head* of the company will talk today	Le *directeur* de la compagnie parlera aujourd'hui
Jim believes he is the *head* of the family	Jim croit qu'il est le *chef* de la famille
The *head* of the institution broke the news	Le *directeur* de l'institution a annoncé la nouvelle

561. *marketing/marketing.*

Jim has joined a *marketing* company	Ji a rejoint une compagnie de *marketing*
The product needs *marketing*	Le produit a besoin de *marketing*
You should study *marketing*	Tu dois étudier le *marketing*

562. *material/matériel*

The *material* is of very high quality.	Le *matériel* est de très haute qualité
I have enough *materials* to build	J'ai assezde *matériaux* pour construire
Use lighter *materials* to construct	Utilise des *matériaux* plus légers pour construire

563. *medical/médical*

Many people have no *medical* insurance.	Beaucoup de gens n'ont pas d'assurance *médicale*
The *medical* board will have a meeting	La commission *médicale* aura une réunion
Did you take the *medical* exam?	As-tu fais l'examen *médical* ?

564. *purpose/but-raison*

What is the *purpose* of your visit?	Quel est le *but* de ta visite ?
The boy came for an unknown *purpose*.	Le garçon est venu pour une *raison* inconnue
The *purpose* of the machine is interesting	Le *but* de la machine est intéressant

565. *question/questionner*

You should not *question* his abilities.	Tu ne dois pas *questionner* ses capacités
I answered all the *questions*	J'ai répondu à toutes les *questions*
How dare you *question* my decision?	Comment oses-tu *questionner* ma décision ?

566. *rock/rock-rocher*

I love *rock*.	J'aime le *rock*
Tom is trying to lift that *rock*.	Tom essaie de soulever ce *rocher*
The big *rock* looks like a castle from afar	Le grand *rocher* ressemble à un château de loin

567. *salt/sel*

The *salt* company is closing down	La compagnie de *sel* ferme
Do not add *salt* in your dishes.	N'ajoute pas le *sel* dans tes plats
High *salt* level in the body is unhealthy	Un haut degré de *sel* dans le corps est mauvais pour la santé

568. *tell/dire*

When time comes, I will *tell* a secret.	Quand le moment viendra, je *dirai* un secret
Do not *tell* lies unnecessarily.	Ne *dis* pas des mensonges unitulement
Tell me your name?	*Dis* moi ton nom ?

569. *themselves/se*

They blamed *themselves* for being wrong.	Il *se* reprochent d'avoir tort
They helped *themselves* to the medicine.	Il *se* sont aidés en médecine
They are going to get *themselves* killed.	Il vont *se* faire tués

570. *traditional/traditionnel*

The family follows *traditional* values.	La famille suit des valeurs *traditionnelles*
The festival has a *traditional* touch	Le festival a une touche *traditionnelle*

The girl belongs to a *traditional* family	La fille appartient à une famille *traitionnelle*

571. *university/université*

Jim will get admitted in the *university.*	Jim sera admis à *l'université*
The professors in the *University* are good	Les professeurs à *l'université* sont bons
I will start working in the *university.*	Je commencerai à travailler à *l'université*

572. *writing/écriture*

The *writing* is on the wall.	*L'écriture* est sur le mur
Your *writing* has a very high standard.	Ton *écriture* a un standard très élevé
Essay *writing* may improve your grammar.	*L'écriture* d'éssai peut améliorer ton grammaire

573. *act/agir*

Try to *act* your age.	Essaie *d'agir* selon ton âge
I will *act* on your advice.	*J'agirai* sur ton conseil
I will *act* as a guide for you.	*J'agirai* comme un guide pour toi

574. *article/article*

This *article* needs to be published tomorrow.	Cet *article* doit être publié demain

The *article* is not controversial.	*L'article* n'est pas controversé
Carry the *article* with you to the office.	Prend *l'article* avec toi à l'office

575. *birth/naissance*

Do you know Jack's date of *birth*?	Connais-tu la date de *naissance* de Jack ?
Do you have your *birth* certificate	As-tu ton certificat de *naissance* ?
The baby birth date was yesterday	La date de *naissance* du bébé était hier

576. *car/voiture*

Jill bought a brand new *car*	Jill a acheté une nouvelle *voiture*
Can you park the *car* in our garage?	Peux-tu garer la *voiture* dans ton garage ?
I need to hire a *car* for tomorrow.	Je dois louer une *voiture* pour demain

577. *cost/coût*

What would be the *cost* of this carpet?	Quel serait le *coût* le coup pour ce tapis ?
Who will bear the *cost* of this damage?	Qui subira le *coût* de ce dégât ?
The *cost* of this furniture is too high	Le *coût* de ce mobilier est très élevé

578. *department/département*

The *department* is very big	Le *département* est très grand

The *department is located* in the University i	Le *département* est situé à l'université
You must inform the concerned *department*	Tu dois informer le *département* concerné

579. *difference/différence*

What *difference* does it make?	Quelle *différence* ça fait ?
There is a *difference.*	Il y a une *différence*
I know the *difference.*	Je connais la *différence*

580. *dog/chien*

I saw a *dog.*	J'ai vu un *chien*
I have a *dog.*	J'ai un *chien*
What a big *dog*!	Quel grand *chien* !

581. *drive/conduire*

She managed to *drive* a car	Elle a réussi à *conduire* une voiture
It is my turn to *drive*	C'est mon tour de *conduire*
I advised him not to *drive.*	Je lui ai conseillé de ne pas *conduire*

582. *exist/existe*

Does God *exist?*	Est-ce que Dieu *existe* ?
I need to know if such law really *exists*	Je dois savoir si une telle loi *existe*

	vraiment
You don't even *exist* in my dreams.	Tu *n'existes* même pas dans mes rêves

583. *federal/fédéral*

Homicide is a *federal* crime	L'homicide est un crime *fédéral*
The *federal* unit has made some changes.	L'unité *fédérale* a fait quelques changements
You need to approach the *federal* court	Tu dois approcher la cour *fédéral*

584. *goal/objectif*

He reached his *goal.*	Il a atteint son *objectif*
He achieved his *goal.*	Il a accompli son *objectif*
He attained his *goal.*	Il est arrivé à son *objectif*

585. *green/vert*

She hates *green* peppers.	Elle déteste le poivron *vert*
We painted the house *green.*	Nous avons peint la maison en *vert*
The dog food is available here	La nourriture du chien est disponible ici

586. *late/tard-retard*

It is *late* already	Il est déjà *tard*

You are *late.*	tu es en *retard*
She is always *late* for school.	Elle est toujours en *retard* pour l'école

587. *news/infos*

Jack had been in the *news* recently	Jack a été dans les *infos* récemment
Did you watch the *news*?	As-tu vu les *infos* ?
I hardly get time to see the *news.*	J'ai difficilement le temps pour regarder les *infos*

588. *object/object*

He hit me with a sharp *object.*	Il m'a frappé avec un *objet* tranchant
The *object* is on the table	*L'objet* est sur la table
The object is now in space	*L'objet* est maintenant dans l'espace

589. *scale/échelle/balance*

Step on the *scale.*	Mets un pas sur *l'échelle*
What is the scale of the disaster?	Quelle est *l'echelle* du désastre
Please put it on the *scale.*	Mets le s'il te plait sur la *balance*

590. *sun/soleil*

The *sun* has gone down.	Le *soleil* s'est couché
The *sun* shone brightly.	Le *soleil* a brillé vivement

The *sun* is up.	Le *soleil* est levé

591.*support/supporter*

I came to *support* Tom.	Je suis venu *supporter* mon équipe
Thanks for the *support.*	Merci pour le *support*
Jill needs your *support.*	Jill a besoin de ton *support*

'592. *Tend/tend*

I *tend* to agree.	Je *tends* à convenir
I *tend* to make mistakes.	Je *tends* à faire des erreurs
I *tend* to agree with Patricia.	Je *tends* à convenir avec Patricia

593. *thus/ainsi*

Thus, making the merger was impossible.	*Ainsi*, faire une fusion était imposible
Thus, they stood until everything was read	*Ainsi*, il sont restés jusqu'à ce que tout soit lu
He *thus* became the Mayor.	Il est *ainsi* devenu le maire

594. *audience/audience*

We had a large *audience*	Nous avons eu une large *audience*
The *audience* was deeply affected	*L'audience* a été profondément affectée

The *audience* clapped a long time	*L'audience* a applaudi longtemps

595. *enjoy/apprécier*

We *enjoy* talking	Nous *apprécions* parler
How did you *enjoy* the movie?	Comment as-tu *apprécié* le film ?
Swimming is one thing I *enjoy*	Nager est une chose que *j'apprécie*

596. *entire/entier*

They spent the *entire* day on the beach.	Ils ont passé le jour *entier* à la plage
The *entire* day was wasted due to rains.	Le jour *entier* était perdu à cause de la pluie
I need a photocopy of the *entire* chapter.	J'ai besoin d'une photocopie du chapitre *entier*

597. *fishing/pêcher*

My father went *fishing*.	Mon père est parti *pêcher*
I suggested that we go *fishing*.	Je suggère qu'on aille *pêcher*
When I was a child I used to go *fishing*	Quand j'étais enfant j'allais *pêcher*

598. *fit/rentrer*

Her camera doesn´t *fit* in her pocket.	Sa caméra ne *rentre* pas dans sa poche
You need trousers that will fit you	Tu as besoin d'un pantalon dans lequel tu *rentreras*

Tom does not fit in the bed	Tom ne *rentres* pas dans le lit

599. *glad/heureux*

I am *glad* that Jill got the job.	Je suis *heureux* que Jill a eu le travail
I am *glad* to see you.	Je suis *heureux* de te voir
I am *glad* to hear that.	Je suis *heureux* d'entendre ça

600. *growth/croissance*

Tom shows a good *growth*	Tom montre une bonne *croissance*
The boy observed her *growth*	Le garçon a observé sa *croissance*
Economic *growth* is very important	La *croissance* économique est très importante

RANKING: 601–700
The most used words

601. Income Revenu	602. Marriage Mariage	603. Note Note	604. Perform Performer	605. Profit Profit
606. Proper Correct	607. Related Apparenté	608. Remove Enlever	609. Rent Louer	610. Return Retourner
611. Run Courrir	612. Speed Vitesse	613. Strong Fort	614. Style Style	615. Throughout A travers
616. User Utilisateur	617. War Guerre	618. Actual Réel	619. Appropriate Approprier	620. Bank Banque
621. Combination Combinaison	622. Complex Complexe	623. Content Content	624. Craft Artisanat	625. Due Dû
626. Easily Facielement	627. Effective Effectif	628. Eventually Finalement	629. Effective Effectif	630. Failure Echec
631. Half Moitié	632. Inside Intérieur	633. Meaning Signification	634. Medicine Médicament	635. Middle Milieu
636. Outside Extérieur	637. Philosophy Philosophie	638. Regular Régulier	639. Reserve Réserve	640. Standard Standard
641. Bus Bus	642. Decide Decide	643. Exchange Echange	644. Eye Oeil	645. Fast Vite
646. Fire Feu	647. Identify Identifier	648. Independent Indépendant	649. Leave Quitter	650. Post Publier
651.	652.	653.	654.	655.

Position Position	Pressure Pression	Reach Atteindre	Rest Repos	Serve Servir
656. Stress Stress	657. Teacher Professeur	658. Watch Montre	659. Wide Large	660. Advantage Avantage
661. Beautiful Beau	662. Benefit Bénéfice	663. Box Boite	664. Charge Charge	665. Communication Communication
666. Complete Complet	667. Continue Continuer	668. Frame Cadre	669. Issue Problème	670. Limited Limité
671. Night Nuit	672. Protect Protéger	673. Require Besoin	674. Significant Signifiant	675. Step Pas
676. Successful Réussi	677. Unless A moins	678. Active Actif	679. Break Briser	680. Chemistry Chimie
681. Cycle Cycle	682. Disease Maladie	683. Disk Disque	684. Electrical Electrique	685. Energy Energie
686. Expensive Cher	687. Face Visage	688. Interested Intéressé	689. Item Objet	690. Metal Métal
691. Nation Nation	692. Negative Négatif	693. Occur Arrive	694. Paint Peinture	695. Pregnant Enceinte
696. Review Réviser	697. Road Route	698. Role Rôle	699. Room Chambre	700. Safe Sûr

601. *income/revenu*

My *income* goes to pay the rent.	Mon *revenu* va pour payer le loyer

My *income* is enough for my family.	Mon *revenu* est assez pour ma famille
You must pay the *income* taxes.	Tu dois payer l'impôt sur le *revenu*

602. *marriage/mariage*

The *marriage* was held at a hotel	Le *mariage* a été tenu dans un hôtel
You must attend the *marriage* party	Tu dois assiter à la fête du *mariage*
The *marriage* procession already departed	Le cortège du *mariage* est déjà parti

603. *note/note*

Take a *note* of the lectures	Prends *note* de la conférence
I need to take a *note* of the expenses.	Je dois prendre *note* des dépenses
Please *note* down the registration number,	*Note* s'il te plait le numéro d'enregistrement

604. *perform/réaliser*

I have an operation to *perform.*	J'ai une opération à *réaliser*
I would love to *perform* a show	J'aimerai *réaliser* un spectacle
You need to *perform* 100 hours of service.	Tu dois *réaliser* 100 heures de service

605. *profit/profit*

You made a *profit.*	Tu as fais un *profit*

I barely make any *profit* now.	Je fais à peine du *profit* maintenant
Tom shared the *profits.*	Tom a partagé le *profit*

606. *proper/adéquat*

Wear a *proper* dress in the evening.	Porte un habit *adéquat* ce soir
You are not carrying *proper* papers.	Tu n'as pas les papiers *adéquats*
The letter arrived in *proper* condition.	La lettre est arrivée dans des conditions *adéquates*

607. *related/apparenté*

These two boys seem to be *related*	Ces garçons ne semblent pas *apparentés*
Are you *related* to that man?	Es-tu *apparenté* à cet homme ?
I don't think you are *related*	Je pense pas que vous êtes *apparentés*

608. *remove/enlève*

Please *remove* the veil in the office	*Enlève* s'il te plait le voile au bureau
Remove makeup before the interview	*Enlève* le maquillage avant l'entretien
You should *remove* all kind of jewelry	Tu dois *enlever* tout genre de bijou

609. *rent/louer-loyer*

This room is for *rent.*	Cette chambre est à *louer*
I would like to *rent* a car.	J'aimerai *louer* une voiture

How much is the *rent* per month?	Combien est le *loyer* par mois ?

610. *return/retour-retourner*

He has reached the point of no *return*.	Il a atteint le point de non *retour*
You should *return* his watch now	Tu lui *retourner* sa montre maintenant
I would like to *return* the books today.	J'aimerais *retourner* les livres aujourd'hui

611. *run/courrir*

I can *run*.	Je peux *courrir*
He began to *run*.	Il a commencé à *courrir*
He likes to *run*.	Om aime *courrir*

612. *speed/accélérer-vitesse*

Speed it up.	*Accélère*
He drove at full *speed*.	Il a conduit à pleine *vitesse*
Speed thrills but kills.	La *vitesse* fait frissoner mais tue

613. *strong/fort*

He is *strong*.	Il est *fort*
He has a *strong* alibi.	Il a un *fort* alibi
My father likes *strong* coffee.	Mon père aime le café *fort*

614. *style/style*

Look at her *style*!	Regarde son *style*
She showed her new dress in a unique *style*	Elle a montré sa nouvelle tenue dans un *style* unique
Her *style* and grace deserve praise.	Son *style* et sa grâce méritent l'éloge

615. *throughout/durant*

He slept *throughout* the day.	Il a dormi *durant* la journée
He studied *throughout* the summer	Il a étudié *durant* l'été
I will work *throughout* the night.	Je travaillerai *durant* la nuit

616. *user/utilisateur*

The *user* details will be changed	Les détails de *l'utilisateur* seront modifiés
Who is the *user* of this workstation?	Qui est *l'utilisateur* de ce poste de travail ?
The settings are *user* defined	Ces paramètres sont définis par *l'utilisateur*

617. *war/guerre*

The *war* finished in 6 days	La *guerre* a fini en 6 jours
Iran and Iraq fought a *war* over 20 years	L'Iran et l'Iraq ont fait la *guerre* pendant 20 ans
The king decided to initiate a *war*	Le roi a décidé d'initier une *guerre*

618. *actual/réel*

The *actual* test results may vary.	Le résultat *réel* du test peut varier
What is your *actual* date of birth?	Quelle est ta date de naissance *réelle*
Here the *actual* photocopy of the document	Voici la photocopie *réelle* du document

619. *appropriate/approprié*

His jokes were not *appropriate*	Sa blaque n'est pas *appropriée*
His dress was not *appropriate*	Son habit n'était pas pas *approprié*
I could not find anything *appropriate*	Je n'ai rien trouvé *d'approprié*

620. *bank/banque*

He went to the *bank.*	Il est allé à la *banque*
Please go to the *bank.*	Va s'il te plait à la *banque*
My brother works in a *bank.*	Mon frère travaile dans un *banque*

621. *combination/combinaison*

Buy a *combination* lock	Achète un cadenas à *combinaison*
You need the correct color *combination*	Tu as besoin de la *combinaison* correct des couleurs
Do you know the right *combination* number	Connais-tu la bonne *combinaison* de chiffres

622. *complex/complexe*

This is a very *complex* situation	C'est une situation très *complexe*
The numerical problems are *complex*	Les problèmes numériques sont *complexes*
Do not make it more *complex* than what it is.	Ne le rend pas plus *complexe* qu'il l'est

623. *content/content*

I am *content* with the rate of progress.	Je suis *content* avec le taux du progrès
Are you *content* with the answer?	Es-tu *content* de la réponse ?
Be *content* with what you have.	Sois *content* avec ce que tu as

624. *craft/artisanat*

The *craft* class will start tomorrow.	La classe *d'artisanat* commencera demain
The required *crafts* are very complex	Les articles *d'artisanat* demandés sont très complexes
This *craft* will be of help	cet *artisanat* sera utile

625. *due/ prévu-dû*

The books are *due* next Monday.	Les livres sont *prévus* la semaine prochaine
In your credit card of five dollars are *due* .	Sur ta carte de crédit 5 dollars sont *dûs*

Jack got his *dues* .	Jack a eu son *dû*

626. *easily/facilement*

Brazil *easily* defeated Germany	Le Brésil a battu *facilement* l'Allemagne
You can *easily* answer these questions.	Tu peux *facilement* répondre à ces questions
You can *easily* reach there in 10 min.	Tu peux *facilement* arriver là-bas en 10 minutes

627. *effective/efficace*

Antibiotics are very *effective*	Les antibiotiques sont très *efficaces*
Effective leadership is not about speeches	Le leadership *efficace* n'est pas que des discours
Sleeping well is *effective* to have a rest	Bien dormir est *efficace* pour se reposer

628. *eventually/finalement*

Tom will forgive her *eventually*.	Tom lui pardonnera *finalement*
I knew Jack would show up *eventually*.	Je sais que Jack va venir *finalement*
You are going to find out *eventually*.	Tu vas découvrir *finalement*

629. *exactly/exactement*

It is *exactly* half-past eight.	Il est *exactement* 8 heures et demi

Tell me *exactly* where he lives.	Dis moi *exactement* ou il habite
He described *exactly* what happened.	Il a décris *exactement* ce qui s'est passé

630. *failure/echec-perte*

Tom blames his *failure* of bad luck.	Tom accuse la mauvaise chance de son *echec*
The city suffered a power *failure.*	La ville a subi une *perte* de courant
This was a massive *failure* government.	C'était un *echec* massif du gouvernement

631. *half/moitié-demi*

I can do it in *half* the time.	Je peux lefaire en la *moitié* du temps
It is almost *half* past eleven.	Il est presque onze heures et *demi*
Half the students did not come	La *moitié* des élèves nesont pas venus

632. *inside/l'intérieur*

They walked *inside.*	Ils ont marché à *l'intérieur*
They peered *inside.*	Ils ont regardé à *l'intérieur*
Please step *inside.*	Rentre s'il te plait à *l'intérieur*

633. *meaning/signification*

What is the *meaning* of all this?	Quelle est la *signification* de tout ça ?
I don't understand the *meaning*	Je ne comprends pas la *signification*

The *meaning* of this letter in unclear	La *signification* de cette lettre est floue

634. *medicine/médicament*

I have to take the *medicine*	Je dois prendrele *médicament*
This *medicine* tastes bitter	Le *médicament* a un goût amer
Take this *medicine* every day	Prends les *médicaments* tous les jours

635. *middle/milieu-intermédiaire*

The girl in the *middle* is beautiful.	La fille au *milieu* est belle
Don't point your *middle* finger to anybody.	Ne pointe ton doigt du *milieu* à personne
Tom acted as a *middle* man	Tom a agi comme *intermédiaire*

636. *outside/l'extérieur*

It is dark *outside*	Il fait noir à *l'extérieur*
It seems warm *outside*	Il fait chaud à *l'extérieur*
Could we have a table *outside*?	Pourrions-nous avoir une table à *l'extérieur* ?

637.*philosophy/philosophie*

Did you study *philosophy* in college?	As-tu étudié la *philosophie* au collège ?
What is his *philosophy* of life?	Quelle est sa *philosophie* dans la vie ?
I need to check the *philosophy*	Je dois vérifier les questions de

questions	*philosophie*

638. *regular/régulier*

The boy had been very *regular*	Le garçon a été très *régulier*
Jill must get *regular* physical training.	Jill doit avoir un entrainement physique *régulier*
Does she go *regularly* to the karate classes?	Va-t-elle *régulièrement* aux séances du karaté ?

639. *reserve/réserver*

I would like to *reserve* a seat.	Je voudrais *réserver* une place
I would like to *reserve* a seat on this bus.	Je voudrais *réserver* une place dans ce bus
I would *reserve* a table for six	Je voudrais *réserver* une table pour six

640. *standard/standars*

The *standard* of education is vey high	Le *standard* d'éducation est très élevé
The *standard* of living went down	Le *standard* de vie a baissé
Jill is now out of *standard* 10.	Jill est maintenant hors du *standard* 10

641. *bus/bus*

Take a *bus.*	Prend un *bus*
He came by *bus.*	Il venu par *bus*

Let us go by *bus*.	Allons par *bus*

642. *decide/décider*

It is up to you to *decide* what to do.	Libre à toi de *décider* quoi faire
You must *decide* the mode of transport	Tu dois *décider* du mode de transport
Decide on your future before it is late.	*Décide* de ton avenir avant qu'il ne soit tard

643. *exchange/échange*

Tom was an ex*change* student	Tom était un étudiant *d'échange*
There was an *exchange* of prisoners	Il y avait un *échange* de prisonniers
Tom is dating an *exchange* student	Tom voit une étudiante *d'échange*

644. *eye/œil-yeux*

There is a large *eye* hospital in London.	C'est un grand hôpital des *yeux* à Londres
The surgery on the left *eye* was successful.	La chirurgie de *l'œil* gauche était réussie
In the storm keep your *eyes* closed.	Dans la tempête garde tes *yeux* fermés

645. *fast/vite rapide*

Lynn runs *fast*.	Lynn court *vite*
My pulse is *fast*.	Mon pouls est *rapide*

Tom can run very *fast.*	Tom peut courir très *vite*

646. *fire/feu*

Do not play with *fire.*	Ne joue pas avec le *feu*
The *fire* is now on	Le *feu* est maintenant allumé
He extinguished the *fire.*	Il a etteint le *feu*

647. *identify/identifier*

Can you *identify* the criminal?	Peux-tu *identifier* le criminel ?
It is very easy to *identify* the boys.	Il est très facile *d'identifier* les garçons
Can you *identify* the man?	Peux-tu *identifier* l'homme ?

648. *independent/indépendant*

The country became *independent* today	Les pays est devenu *indépendant* aujourd'hui
Ireland is now an *independent* nation.	L'Irlande est maintenant une nation *indépendante*
I want be *independent* in my life.	Je veux être *indépendant* dans ma vie

649. *leave/quitter*

I will *leave* you for a long time	Je te *quitterai* pour un long moment
When did you *leave* office?	Quand as-tu *quitté* le bureau ?

I need to speak to her before I *leave*.	Je dois lui parler avant que je *quitte*

650. *post/poste*

Tom reached the top *post* in his company.	Tom a atteint le plus haut *poste* dans sa compagnie
The minister was removed from the *post*	Le ministre a été retiré de son *poste*
The *post* is still available	Le *poste* est toujours disponible

651. *position/position*

What *position* do you play?	Dans quelle *position* joues-tu ?
I have made my *position* clear.	J'ai rendu ma *position* claire
Take your *position*.	Prend ta *position*

652. *pressure/pression*

I have high blood *pressure*.	J'ai une hyper*tension* sanguine
If bleeding, put *pressure* on the wound.	Si tu saignes, fais une *pression* sur la plaie
The water *pressure* burst the pipe	La *pression* de l'eau a cassé le tuyau

653. *reach/atteindre*

Can you *reach* the ceiling?	Peux-tu *atteindre* le toit ?
The ball is out of his *reach*	Le ballon est hors *d'atteinte*

You must *reach* the train	Tu dois *atteindre* le train

654. *rest/reposer*

Let us *rest* here	*Reposons*-nous
May I take a *rest*?	Puis-je me *reposer* ?
I had a good night's *rest*	J'ai eu une bonne nuit de *repos*

655. *serve/servir*

Please *serve* the drinks inmediatamente	*Sers* s'il te plait les boisson tout de suite
You should always *serve* with a smile.	Tu dois toujours *servir* avec le sourire
To *serve* in a restaurant is a skill	*Servir* dans un restaurant est une compétence

656. *stress/stress*

Jim is under huge *stress*	Jim subit un grand *stress*
Aerobics relieves *stress*	L'aérobique soulage le *stress*
Do not take too much *stress*	Ne te mets pas trop de *stress*

657. *teacher/professeur*

He is a *teacher.*	Il est *professeur*
I was a *teacher.*	J'étais *professeur*
My father is a *teacher.*	Mon père est *professeur*

658. *watch/montre*

The *watch* looks very beautiful	La *montre* semble très belle
He always wears a Rolex *watch*	Il porte toujours une *montre* Rolex
The leather strap of the *watch* está rota	La sangle en cuir de la *montre* est cassée

659. *wide/large*

The road leading to the house is very *wide.*	La route menant à la maison est très *large*
Our knowledge is very *wide*	Notre savoir est très *large*
The river coast is *wide*	La côte de la rivière est très *large*

660. *advantage/avantage*

The boy had a distinct *advantage* over Tom	Le garçon a un grand *avantage* sur Tom
Always take *advantage* of any situation	Prends toujours *l'avantage* de toute situation
Italy enjoyed the home *advantage* against	L'Italie a profité de *l'avantage* de la maison

661. *Beautiful/beau*

Jill is very *beautiful.*	Jill est très *belle*
The lake looks *beautiful* from a	Le lac semble *beau* de loin

distance.	
Cheryl has *beautiful* hair.	Cheryl a de *beaux* cheuveux

662. *benefit/bénéfice*

The umpire granted the *benefit* of doubt.	L'arbitre a accordé le *bénéfice* du doute
This is for your *benefit.*	Ceci est pour ton *bénéfice*
This law will *benefit* the poor.	Cette loi *bénéficiera* au pauvre

663. *box/boite*

How do you make a *box*?	Comment fais-tu une *boite* ?
This *box* contains apples.	Cette *boite* contient des pommes
Why did you open the *box*?	Pourquoi as-tu ouvert la *boite* ?

664. *charge/frais*

Food and drinks is free of *charge.*	La nourriture et les boissons sont sans *frais*
Charge it to my account.	Mets les *frais* sur mon compte
Do you *charge* for delivery?	Factures-tu des *frais* pour la livraison ?

665. *communication/communication*

The *communication* has improved a lot.	La *communication* s'est beaucoup améliorée

The *communication* towers are high	Les tours des *communication* sont hautes
You need to improve your *communication*	Tu dois améliorer ta *communication*

666. *complete/complet*

The project is *complete*	Le projet est *complet*
Jill should *complete* his work first	Jill doit d'abord *compléter* son travail
Did you *complete* the work?	As-tu *complété* le travail ?

667. *continue/continuer*

I cannot *continue* on this project	Je ne peux pas *continuer* le projet
You must *continue* on your journey	Tu doins *continuer* dans ton voyage
Please *continue* with your work.	*Continue* s'il te plait avec ton travail

668. *frame/cadre*

The photo *frame* was broken	Le *cadre* de la photo était cassé
Please *frame* this lovely photo	*Encadre* s'il te plait cette belle photo
The door *frame* will be changed	Le *cadre* de la porte sera changé

669. *issue/problème*

This *issue* needs to be solved now	Le *problème* doit être résolu maintenant

This *issue* is blown out of proportions	Le *problème* est disproportionné
This is no *issue* at all.	Ce n'est pas un *problème* du tout

670. *limited/limité*

They serve food in *limited* quantities	Il servent la nourriture en quantité *limitée*
The calls are *limited* to one minute	Les appels sont *limités* à une minute
The internet speed is 4 Mbps only.	La vitesse d'internet est de 4 Mbps seulement

671.*night/nuit*

It happened during the *night*	C'est arrivé pendant la *nuit*
How was your *night*?	Comment était ta *nuit* ?
I stayed up all *night*.	Je suis resté toute la *nuit*

672. *protect/protéger*

Tom must *protect* his younger brother	Tom doit *protéger* son petit frère
The government must *protect* the species.	Le gouvernement doit *protéger* les espèces
We will *protect* you.	Nous te *protégerons*

673. *require/besoin*

You *require* a new pair of shoes.	Tu as *besoin* d'une nouvelle paire de

	chaussures
I *require* a new set of books	J'ai *besoin* d'une nouvelle série de livres
I think I *require* a new golf club.	Je pense que j'ai *besoin* d'un nouveau club de golf

674. *significant/signifiant*

This deal is very *significant* for country	L'accord est très *signifiant* pour le pays
What you did there was very *significant*	Ce que tu as fais là était très *sisgnifiant*
Today is a *significant* day in my life	Aujourd'hui est un jour *signifiant* dans ma vie

675. *step/marche-pas*

Watch your *step*.	Fais attention à la *marche*
Please *step* aside.	Fais un *pas* de côté s'il te plait
Do not *step* on the broken glass.	Ne *marche* pas sur le verre brisé

676. *successful/réussi*

The concert was *successful*.	Le concert était *réussi*
They won't be *successful*.	Il ne *réussiront* pas
Tom seemed *successful*.	Tom semble avoir *réussi*

677. *unless/à moins*

Unless you come to the show, I will sing.	*A moins* que vous veniez au spectacle, je chanterai
I´ll be angry *unless* you attend my wedding,	Je serai furieux *à moins* que tu viennes à mon mariage
Unless you come to my house, I will not eat.	*A moins* que tu viennes à ma maison, je ne magerai pas

678. *active/actif*

The baby is very *active* in nature.	Le bébé est de natur très *actif*
You must remain *active* throughout the day.	Tu dois rester *actif* toute la journée
You must lead an *active* lifestyle	Tu dois mener un style de vie *actif*

679. *break/briser*

You need to play games to *break* monotony.	Tu dois jouer des jeux pour *briser* la monotonie
Put the glass on the table without breaking it	Mets le verre sur la table sans le *briser*
If you *break* it you pay it	Si tu le *brises*, tu le paies

680. *chemistry/chimie*

You need to take *chemistry* lessons	Tu dois prendre des leçons de *chimie*
The questions on *chemistry* were tough.	Les questions en *chimie* étaient difficiles
The *chemistry* between them was	La *chimie* entre eux était manquante

missing.	

681. *cycle/cycle*

Every work has a *cycle*	Tout travail a un *cycle*
My *cycle* is over	Mon *cycle* est terminé
The year has four cycles	L'année a quatre *cycles*

682. *disease/enfermedad*

He died of the *disease.*	Il est mort de la *maladie*
Mumps is an infectious *disease.*	Les oreillons est une *maladie* infectueuse
The *disease* spreads very quickly.	La *maladie* se répand rapidement

683. *disk/disque*

The boy returned the floppy *disk*	Le garçon a retourné le *disque*
The *disk* is now an obsolete item.	Le *disque* est maintenant un objet obsolète
You need a car with *disk* brakes.	Tu as besoin d'une voiture avec des freins à *disque*

684. *electrical/électrique*

The *electrical* wire broke in the storm.	Le cable *électrique* a cassé lors de la tempête

She graduated as *electrical* engineer	Elle est diplomée comme ingénieure *électrique*
You need to re-do the *electrical* wiring	Tu dois refaire le cablage *électrique*

685. *energy/énergie*

The *energy* is always available.	*L'énergie* est toujours disponible
I need glucose to lift my *energy*.	J'ai besoin du glucose pour hausser mon *énergie*
Tom is always full of *energy*	Tom est toujours plein *d'énergie*

686. *expensive/chère*

Tom gave her a very *expensive* watch	Tom lui a donné une montre très *chère*
The rooms at this hotel are *expensive*	Les chambres dans cet hôtel sont très *chères*
This is a very *expensive* piece of jewelry	C'est une très *chère* pièce de bijouterie

687. *face/visage*

You must wash your *face* twice a day	Tu dois laver ton *visage* deux fois par jour
The *face* mask was on the floor	Le masque du *visage* était sur le sol
Your *face* is smeared with dust	Ton *visage* est endui de poussière

688. *interested/intéressé*

Are you *interested* in ancient history?	Es-tu *intéressé* par l'histoire ancienne
Are you *interested* in the job?	Es-tu *intéressé* par le travail ?
I am not *interested* in her at all.	Je ne suis pas *intéressé* par elle du tout

689. *item/objet*

Did you pack that *item*?	As-tu emballé *l'objet* ?
The police collected each *item* as evidence.	La police a collecté chaque *objet* comme preuve
Did you clean the *item*?	As-tu nettoyé *l'objet* ?

690. *metal/métal*

The *metal* rod pierced her body	La tige du *métal* a percé son corps
The car is made with *metal*	La voiture est faite de *métal*
The *metal* door needs to be cleaned	La porte en *métal* doit être nettoyée

691. *nation/nation*

Switzerland is known to be a neutral *nation*	La suisse est connue pour être une *nation* neutre
You must always love your *nation*	Tu dois toujours aimer ta *nation*
The *nation* should be protected	La *nation* doit être protégé

692. *negative/negative*

Tom has a *negative* approach	Tom a une approche *négative*

Do you harbor *negative* thoughts.	Cultives-tu des pensées *négatives* ?
Did you bring the *negative* with you?	As-tu apporté le *négatif* avec toi ?

693. *occur/arrive*

Did this idea *occur* to you?	Est-ce que cette idée *t'arrive ?*
The meeting should *occur* within 2 days.	La réunion *arrivera* dans 2 jours
How did it *occur* to you?	Comment est-ce *arrivé* à toi ?

694. *paint/peinture*

The exterior *paint* has come off.	La *peinture* extérieure est tombée
You need to *paint* the bedrooms!	Tu dois *peindre* les chambres
The *paint* is of inferior quality.	La *peinture* est d'une qualité inférieure

695. *pregnant/enceinte*

My wife became *pregnant* again	Mon épouse est tombée *enceinte* de nouveau
Jill became *pregnant* after 5 years	Jill est tombée *enceinte* après 5 ans
Are you pregnant ?	Es-tu *enceinte* ?

696. *review/réviser*

The game rules needs to be *reviewed*	Les règles du jeu doivent être *révisées*
You should *review* this movie right	Tu dois *réviser* le film tout de suite

away	
Do you *review* vintage cars?	*Révises*-tu les anciennes voitures ?

697. *road/route*

This is a *road* map.	C'est une carte de *route*
This *road* leads to the park.	La *route* mène au parc
She told us the *road* was closed.	Elle nous a dit que la *route* était fermée

698. *role/rôle*

The girl was chosen for the leading *role*	La fille était choisie pour le *rôle* principal
This *role* is tailor-made for you	Ce *rôle* t'est fait sur mesure
I love *role* playing games	J'aime les jeux de *rôle*

699. *room/chambre*

The *room* is very big.	La *chambre* est très grande
My *room* is very airy.	Ma *chambre* est très aérée
Where is your *room*?	Où est ta *chambre* ?

700. *safe/sûre*

This house is very *safe*	Cette maison est très *sûre*
The area is not *safe* for single women	Le secteur n'est pas *sûr* pour les femmes seules

Singapore is a very *safe* place	Singapour est un lieu très *sûr*

RANKING: 701–800
The most used words

701. Screen Ecran	702. Soup Soupe	703. Stay Rester	704. Structure Structure	705. View Vue
706. Visit Visiter	707. Visual Visuel	708. Write Ecrire	709. Wrong Mauvais	710. Account Compte
711. Advertising Publier	712. Affect Affecter	713. Ago Il y a	714. Anyone Personne	715. Approach Approcher
716. Avoid Eviter	717. Ball Balle	718. Behind Au-delà	719. Certainly Certainement	720. Concerned Inquiet
721. Cover Couvrir	722. Discipline Discipline	723. Location Location	724. Medium Moyen	725. Normally Normalement
726. Prepare Préparer	727. Quick Rapide	728. Ready Prêt	729. Report Rapport	730. Rise Lever
731. Share Partager	732. Success Succès	733. Addition Addition	734. Apartment Appartement	735. Balance Balance
736. Bit Peu	737. Black Noir	738. Bottom Bas	739. Build Construire	740. Choice Choix
741. Education Education	742. Gift Cadeau	743. Impact Impact	744. Machine Machine	745. Math Math
746. Moment Moment	747. Painting Peinture	748. Politics Politique	749. Shape Forme	750. Straight Direct/Droit
751.	752.	753.	754.	755.

Tool Outil	Walk Marcher	White Blanc	Wind Vent	Achieve Accomplir
756. Address Adresse	757. Attention Attention	758. Average Moyen	759. Believe Croire	760. Beyond Au-delà
761. Career Carrière	762. Culture Culture	763. Decision Décision	764. Direct Direct	765. Event Evènement
766. Excellent Excellent	767. Extra Plus	768. Intelligent Intelligent	769. Interesting Intéressant	770. Junior Junior
771. Morning Matin	772. Pick Selectionner	773. Poor Pauvre	774. Pot Pot	775. Pretty Joli
776. Property Propriété	777. Receive Recevoir	778. Seem Semble	779. Shopping Shopping	780. Sign Signe
781. Student Etudiant	782. Table Table	783. Task Tache	784. Unique Unique	785. Wood Bois
786. Anything Rien	787. Classic Classique	788. Competition Compétition	789. Condition Condition	790. Contact Contact
791. Credit Crédit	792. Currently Actuellement	793. Discuss Discuter	794. Distribution Distribuer	795. Egg Oeuf
796. Entertainment Divertissement	797. Final Final	798. Happy Heureux	799. Hope Espérer	800. Ice Glace

701. *screen/l'écran*

The *screen* on the TV has been	*L'écran* de la télévision a été

damaged	endommagé
You need a new LCD *screen* for your desktop	Tu as besoin d'un nouvel *écran* LCD pour ton bureau
Always check the video *screen*	Vérifie toujours *l'écran* vidéo

702. *soup/soupe*

The *soup* was delicious	La *soupe* était délicieuse
I ordered four kinds of *soup* for lunch	J'ai commandé quatre types de *soupes* pour le déjeuner
Order a bowl of *soup* for the child	Commande un bol de *soupe* pour l'enfant

703. *stay/reste*

I will *stay* at home	Je *resterai* à la maison
Stay here with us	*Reste* ici avec nous
He had to *stay* in bed	Il devait *rester* au lit

704. *structure/structure*

The *structure* of the building is destroyed	La *structure* du bâtiment est détruite
This *structure* is totally illegal	La *structure* est totalement illégale
The *structure* is seventy feet high	La *structure* fait soixante-dix pieds de hauteur

705. *view/vue-voir*

The *view* from the top is amazing.	La *vue* du haut est géniale
I can easily *view* the hotel from here	Je peux facilement *voir* l'hôtel d'ici
Did you have a good *view* of the skyline?	As-tu une bonne *vue* de l'horizon ?

706. *visit/visiter*

He will *visit* his uncle	Il *visitera* son oncle
She did not *visit* anybody	Elle n'a *visité* personne
Her dream is to *visit* Paris	Son rêve est de *visiter* Paris

707. *visual/visuel*

The *visual* effects in the movie were nice	Les effets *visuels* dans le film étaient jolis
The *visual* clues were very helpful	Les signes *visuels* étaient très utiles
This is a *visual* image of the home	C'est une image *visuelle* de la maison

708. *write/écrire*

Always *write* correct English	*Ecris* toujours un Anglais correct
Write a letter to your mom	*Ecris* une lettre à ta maman
Did you *write* the resignation letter?	As-tu *écris* la lettre de démission ?

709. *wrong/tort-mauvais*

I was *wrong*.	J'avais *tort*
I got on the *wrong* bus.	J'ai pris le *mauvais* bus
It is *wrong* to tell a lie.	C'est *mauvais* de dire un mensonge

710. *account/compte*

I paid my holiday on your *account*	J'ai payé mes vacances sur ton *compte*
John has a closed bank *account*	John a un *compte* bancaire fermé
Open a bank *account* tomorrow	Ouvre un *compte* bancaire demain

711. *advertising/publication-publicité*

The *advertising* board convened a meeting	Le conseil de *publication* a convenu d'un réunion
You must report to the *advertising* council	Tu dois informer le conseil de *publication*
The brand needs aggressive *advertising*	La marque a besoin d'une *publicité* agressive

712. *affect/affecter*

The news should not *affect* her at all	Les infos ne doivent pas *l'affecter* du tout
Earthquakes *affect* a wide area	Les tremblements de terre *affectent* une large zone
The new timetable will *affected*	Le nouveau programme sera *affecté*

713. *ago/il y a*

He died one year *ago*	Il est mort *il y a* un an
It happened a long time *ago*	C'est arrivé *il y a* longtemps
She met him three years *ago*	Elle l'a rencontré *il y a* trois ans

714. *anyone/personne*

Do not tell *anyone* this	Ne le dis à *personne*
Don't share this with *anyone*	Ne partage ça avec *personne*
There isn't *anyone* in the room	Il n'y a *personne* dans la chambre

715. *approach/approche*

This is not the proper *approach*	Ce n'est pas la bonne *approche*
You have to change your *approach*	Tu dois changer ton *approche*
Approach the problem differently	*Approche* le problème différemment

716. *avoid/éviter*

I *avoid* traveling by air	*J'évite* de voyager par les airs
There are a few problems we can *avoid*	Il y a plusieurs problèmes que nous pouvons *éviter*
We took the plain to *avoid* traffic	Nous avons pris l'avion pour *éviter* le traffic

717. *ball-balle*

He threw the *ball.*	Il a lancé la *balle*
He kicked the *ball.*	Il a frappé la *balle*
Roll the *ball* to me.	Fais rouler la *balle* vers moi

718. *behind/derrière*

I am *behind* him	Je suis *derrière* lui
Look *behind* you	Regarde *derrière* toi
It is *behind* the wall	C'est *derrière* le mur

719. *certainly/certainement*

I *certainly* don't regret this trip	Je ne regrette *certainement* pas ce voyage
I was *certainly* not a part of the team.	Je n'étais *certainement* pas un membre de l'équipe
This will *certainly* make a huge difference.	Ça va *certainement* faire une grande différence

720. *concerned/inquiet*

I was *concerned* for Sophie and his child	J'étais *inquiet* pour Sophie et son enfant
I was *concerned* about my pet dog	J'étais *inquiet* à propos de mon chiot
I am *concerned* because the deal is over	Je suis *inquiet* parce que l'accord est fini

721. *cover/couvrir*

You should *cover* the garbage	Tu devrais *couvrir* les déchets
Let us *cover* up these fireworks	Allons *couvrir* les feux d'artifice
One thousand dollars will *cover* all expenses.	Mille dollars *couvriront* les dépenses

722. *discipline/discipline*

You have to maintain the *discipline*	Tu dois maintenir la *discipline*
Discipline will make us better in life	La *discpline* nous rendra meilleurs dans la vie
Discipline is more important	La *discipline* est très importante

723. *location/emplacement*

The mall is in a very good *location.*	Le mall est dans un très bon *emplacement*
Did you find the *location* of the building?	As-tu trouvé *l'emplacement* de l'immeuble ?
The hotel has an excellent *location.*	L'hôtel a un excellent *emplacement*

724. *medium/moyen-médium*

The box is of *medium* size	La boite est de taille *moyenne*
She worked as a *medium* for many years	Elle a travaillé comme *médium* plusieurs années
He used water colors as the sole	Il a utilisé les couleurs à l'eau comme

medium	seul *moyen*

725. *normally/normalement*

Normally, I never do this	*Normalement*, je n'ai jamais fais ça
Can you do that *normally*?	Peux-tu faire ça *normalement*
It was not something I would *normally* do	Ce n'était pas une chose que je ferais *normalement*

726. *prepare/préparer*

I need to *prepare* for the exams	Je dois me *préparer* pour l'examen
Did you *prepare* well for the big event?	As-tu bien *préparé* pour le grand évènement ?
I need milk to *prepare* breakfast	J'ai besoin du lait pour *préparer* le petit-déjeuner

727. *quick/rapide*

The boy was *quick* to learn	L'enfant apprenait *rapidement*
Jim is very *quick* on his feet.	Jim est très *rapide* à pieds
He was *quick* to point out the mistakes.	Il pointait *rapidement* les erreurs

728. *ready/prêt*

The king was *ready* for the battle	Le roi était *prêt* pour la bataille

The team was *ready* for its first match	L'équipe était *prête* pour son premier match
I am *ready* to die for the country	Je suis *prêt* à mourir pour le pays

729. *report/rapport*

Please *report* this to the police	*Rapporte* ça s'il te plait à la police
Submit the *report* as soon as possible	Envoie le *rapport* dès que possible
Where is the police *report*?	Où est le *rapport* de police

730. *rise/lever*

I am sure Jim will *rise*	Je suis sûr que Jim va se *lever*
To *rise* early is a healthy habit	Se *lever* tôt est un habitude saine
I need to *rise* early tomorrow	Je dois me *lever* tôt demain

731. *share/partager*

Please *share* the details with us	*Partage* s'il te plait les détails avec nous
I always *share* the food with my friends.	Je *partage* toujours la nourriture avec mes amis
Did you *share* your bank password?	As-tu *partagé* ton mot de passe de banque ?

732. *success/succès*

The team enjoyed moderate *success*	L'auipe a apprécié le *succès* modéré
Jack was a real *success* on the tour	Jack était un vrai *succès* dans le tour
You will have a *success* this year.	Tu auras du *succès* cette année

733. *addition/addition*

There has been no *addition* to the final list	Il n'a ya pas eu *d'addition* à la liste finale
In *addition* you must carry your certificate	En *addition*, tu dois amener ton certificat
The boy is very good for *additions*	L'enfant est très bon en *addition*

734. *apartment/appartement*

The *apartment* is really beautiful	*L'appartement* est très beau
You spent a fortune on this *apartment*	Tu as dépensé une fortune dans cet *appartement*
Did you sell your old *apartment*?	As-tu vendu ton viel *appartement* ?

735. *balance/ balance/bilan*

Do you have *balance* in your cell phone?	As-tu une *balance* sur ton téléphone ?
The *balance* sheet looks dubious.	La feuille du *bilan* semble douteuse
Check the *balance* before leaving the office	Vérifie la *balance* avant de quitter le bureau

736. *bit/peu*

He has changed a *bit* since sixth grade.	Il a changé un *peu* depuis la sixième
I need to work on it *bit* by *bit.*	Je dois travailler dessus *peu* à *peu*
Do a *bit* and wait for the results.	Fais un *peu* et attends les résultats

737. *black/noir*

The coat is *black*	Le manteau est *noir*
I will wear a *black* suit to the funeral	Je mettrai une tenue *noire* pour les funérailles
He bought a *black* Cadillac on her birthday	Il a acheté une cadillac *noire* pour son anniversaire

738. *bottom/bas*

The camp is located at the *bottom*	Le camp est situé en *bas*
The *bottom* is very loose.	Le *bas* est très instable
Check the *bottom* of the drawer	Vérifie le *bas* du tiroir

739. *build/construire*

You need to *build* a bridge	Tu dois *construire* un pont
I need to *build* a new cage	Je dois *construire* une nouvelle cage
Birds *build* nests.	Les oiseaux *construisent* des nids

740. *choice/choix*

Make your *choice.*	Fais ton *choix*
We have a wide *choice* of books.	Nous avons un large *choix* de livres
He had no *choice* but to run away.	Il n'a pas d'autre *choix* que fuire

741. *education/Education*

The standard of *education* is very high	Le standard *d'éducation* est très elevé
Send her to England for *education.*	Envoie-là en Angleterre pour *l'éducation*
A good *education* is very important	Une bonne *éducation* est très importante

742. *gift/regalo*

He accepted her *gift.*	Il a accepté son *cadeau*
She will offer him a *gift.*	Elle lui offrira un *cadeau*
Tom brought Mary a *gift.*	Tom a apporté un *cadeau* à Mary

743. *impact/impact*

Prepare yourselves for an *impact.*	Prépare toi pour un *impact*
The storm had an *impact* on the crops.	La tempête a un *impact* sur les cultures
The *impact* of science is great.	*L'impact* de la sicence est génial

744. *machine/machine*

I bought a new sewing *machine*	J'ai acheté une nouvelle *machine* à coudre
I don't know how to use this *machine*	Je ne sais pas comment utiliser cette *machine*
I asked her turn on the *machine*	Je lui ai demandé d'allumer la *machine*

745. *math/math*

His performance in *math* is bad	Sa performance en *math* est très mauvaise
Did you do your *math* homework?	As-tu fais ton test de *math* ?
I am very weak in on *math*	Je suis très faible en *math*

746. *moment/moment*

Wait a *moment*	Attend un *moment*
Be quiet for a *moment*	Sois calme pour un *moment*
I am busy at the *moment*	Je suis occupé pour le *moment*

747. *painting/peinture*

Jim is very good at *painting* portraits	Jim est très bon dans la *peinture* des protraits
I loved her new *painting* of the kitten	J'ai aimé sa nouvelle *peinture* du chaton
We went to see some old *paintings*	Nous commes allés voir quelques vielles *peintures*

748. *politics/politique*

I hate *politics*	Je déteste la *politique*
He has no interest in *politics*	Il n'a aucun intérpet pour la *politique*
Mary will enter in *politics*	Maru entrera dans la *politique*

749. *shape/forme*

Jim looks in excellent *shape*	Jim semble en excellente *forme*
What is the *shape* of that box?	Quelle est la *forme* de cette boite ?
You look terribly out of *shape.*	Tu sembles terriblement hors de *forme*

750. *straight/droit direct*

Sit up *straight*	Assis-toi *droit*
Give it to me *straight*	Donne le moi *direct*
He drew a *straight* line with his pencil	Il a dessiné une ligne *droite* avec son crayon

751. *tool/outil*

You need proper *tools*	Tu as besoin *d'outils* corrects
Did you buy new *tools*?	M'as-tu acheté de nouveaux *outils* ?
Where is your *tool* kit?	Où est ta boite à *outils* ?

752. *walk/marche*

I *walk* whenever I can	Je *marche* dès que je peux

I *walk* to school.	Je *marche* à l'école
Walk ahead of me.	*Marche* devant moi

753. *white/blanc*

It is all *white.*	Il est *blanc*
The dog is *white.*	Le chien est *blanc*
It is perfectly *white.*	C'est parfaitement *blanc*

754. *wind/vent*

The *wind* has grown stronger	Le *vent* devient plus fort
The *wind* has died down	Le *vent* s'est calmé
The *wind* blew every morning	Le *vent* souffle chaque matin

755. *achieve/accomplir*

This man has nothing left to *achieve*	L'homme n'a rien laissé à *accomplir*
To become famous, you need to *achieve* a lot.	Pour devnir célèbre, tu dois beaucoup *accomplir*
It´s great you could *achieve* your goals	C'est génial que tu puisses *accomplir* tes objectifs ?

756. *address/adresse*

Can I have your *address*?	Puis-je avoir ton *adresse* ?
Here is the *address*	Voici *l'adresse*

I forgot his *address*	J'ai oublié *l'adresse*

757.*attention/attention*

May I have your *attention*, please?	Puis-je avoir votre *attention* ?
The boy demanded undivided *attention*	L'enfant demande toute *l'attention*
You must pay *attention* in class	Tu dois faire *attention* en classe

758. *average/moyen*

His results were only *average*	Ses résultats étaient seulement *moyens*
His *average* score was 56	Son score *moyen* était 56
I am hoping for an *average* result	J'espère un résultat *moyen*

759. *believe/croire*

I *believe* you	Je te *crois*
I *believe* in him	Je *crois* en lui
To see is to *believe*	Voir c'est *croire*

760. *beyond/au-delà*

It is *beyond* me	C'est *au-delà* de moi
He is *beyond* hope	Il est *au-delà* de l'espoir
My house is *beyond* that bridge	Ma maison est *au-delà* de ce pont

761. *career/carrière*

You need a new *career*	Tu as besoin d'une nouvelle *carrière*
You are risking your *career*	Tu risques ta *carrière*
I have my *career* to think of	Je dois penser à ma *carrière*

762. *culture/culture*

Foreign *cultures* are interesting	Les *cultures* étrangères sont intéressantes
I love French *culture*	J'aime la *culture* française
Culture is based on language.	*La culture* est basée sur la langue

763. *decision/décision*

You must make a *decision* soon	Tu dois prendre une *décision* bientôt
The final *decision* is yours	La *décision* finale est à toi
I need to take a final *decision*	Je dois prendre une *décision* finale

764. *direct/direct*

He made a *direct* accusation.	Il a fait une accusation *directe*
There is a *direct* train to London	Il y a un train *direct* vers Londres
Is there any *direct* flight to Hong Kong?	Y a-t-il des vols *directs* vers Hong Kong ?

765. *event/l'évènement*

I won the *event*	J'ai gagné *l'évènement*
We postponed the *event*	Nous avons reporté *l'évènement*
Tom accompanied Mary to the *event*	Tom a accompagné Mary à *l'évènement*

766. *excellent/excellent*

That is *excellent.*	C'est *excellent*
Tom is an *excellent* manager	Tom est un *excellent* gérant
This is *excellent* news	C'est une *excellente* information

767. *extra/en plus*

We have no *extra* money	Nous n'avons pas de l'argent *en plus*
You may need an *extra* blanket	Tu aurais besoin d'une couverture *en plus*
Do you have an *extra* pen?	As-tu un stylo *en plus* ?

768. *intelligent/intelligent*

Jim is very *intelligent.*	Jim est très *intelligent*
Mary is more *intelligent* than Jack.	Mary est plus *intelligent* que Jack
Cheryl made an *intelligent* decision.	Cheryl a pris une décision *intélligente*

769. *interesting/intéressante*

This is an *interesting* novel	C'est une nouvelle *intéressante*
The premise of the book is very	La prémisse du livre est très

interesting	*intéressante*
The movie has an *interesting* storyline	Le film a une intrigue *intéressante*

770. *junior/jeune-secondaire*

The boy studies in *junior* school.	Le garçon étudie à l'école *secondaire*
I am a *junior* in high school.	Je suis un *jeune* à l'université
I teach French at a *junior* school.	J'enseigne le Français à l'école *secondaire*

771. *morning/matin*

I came home this *morning.*	Je suis venu à la maison ce *matin*
There was a bomb attack in the *morning.*	Il y avait une attaque à la bombe ce *matin*
Did you catch the *morning* train?	As-tu attrapé le train du *matin* ?

772. *pick/sélectionner*

Ronaldo was *picked* best player	Ronaldo a été *sélctionné* comme meilleur joueur
I will *pick* the mail tonight	Je *sélectionnerai* le courrier ce soir
Can you please *pick* the photo?	Peux-tu s'il te plait *sélectionner* la photo ?

773. *poor/pauvre*

Tom is very *poor*	Tom est très *pauvre*
Sudan is a *poor* country.	Le Soudan est un pays *pauvre*
I always help the *poor.*	J'aide toujours les *pauvres*

774. *pot/pot*

The *pot* is full of soup	Le *pot* est plein de soupe
I will make a *pot* of coffee.	Je ferai un *pot* de café
Is there any water in the *pot*?	Y a-t-il de l'eau dans le *pot* ?

775. *pretty/joli*

Mary looks *pretty* in the new dress	Mary est *jolie* dans la nouvelle robe
I have a *pretty* looking doll	J'ai une *jolie* pouppée
Her books are *pretty*	Ses livres sont *jolis*

776. *property/propriété*

He inherited a huge *property*	Il a hérité une enorme *propriété*
My *property* is being valued by the bank	Ma *propriété* est valorisée par la baque
He couldn´t pay and lost the *property*	Il pouvait pas payer et perdre la *propriété*

777. *receive/reçu*

Did you *receive* my letter?	As-tu *reçu* ma lettre ?

I did not *receive* even one letter from him.	Je n'aime même pas *reçu* une lettre de lui
Did you *receive* the offer letter?	As-tu *reçu* la lettre de proposition ?

778. *seem/semble*

You *seem* busy	Tu *sembles* occupé
I *seem* to be lost	Je *semble* être perdu
I *seem* to have a fever	Je *semble* avoir une fièvre

779. *shopping/shopping*

Mary will go for *shopping* today	Mary ira aujourd'hui pour faire du *shopping*
There are many *shopping* malls in Boston	Il y a beaucoup de malls de *shopping* à boston
Women generally prefer *shopping* not alone	Les femmes préfèrent généralement faire le *shopping* accompagnées

780. *sign/signe*

It is a *sign* of bad times	C'est un *signe* du mauvais temps
Did you check the *sign* post?	As-tu vérifié le *signe* ?
It is a clear *sign* of troubles	C'est un *signe* clair de problèmes

781. *student/étudiant*

She is a *student*	Elle est *étudiante*
Tom is a very good *student*	Tom est un très bon *étudiant*
He is a university *student*	Il est un *étudiant* d'université

782. *table/table*

That is a *table*	C'est une *table*
I hid under the *table*	Je me suis caché sous la *table*
This *table* is not steady	Cette *table* n'est pas stable

783. *task/tâche*

Mary was not up to the *task*	Mary n'a pas rempli sa *tâche*
Did you complete your school *task*?	As-tu terminé tes *tâches* à l'école ?
It is tough *task.*	C'est une *tâche* difficile

784. *unique/unique*

The flowers have a *unique* smell	Les fleurs ont une odeur *unique*
Each citizen has a *unique* card	Chaque citoyen a une carte *unique*
There is nothing *unique* in the museum	Il n'y a rien *d'unique* dans le musée

785. *wood/bois*

That toy is made of *wood*	Le jouet est fait de *bois*
The desk is made of *wood*	Le bureau est fait de *bois*

Wood floats but iron sinks	Le *bois* flotte mais l'écier coule

786. *anything/rien*

I cannot see *anything*	Je ne peux *rien* voir
I do not know *anything*	Je ne connais *rien*
Please don´t take *anything*	Ne prends *rien* s'il te plait

787.*classic/classique*

This is a *classic* film	C'est un film *classique*
Do you have any *classic*?	As-tu un *clasique* ?
This scene is considered a *classic*	Cette scène est considérée comme un *classique*

788. *competition/compétition*

There is stiff *competition* between the two	Il y a une rude *compétition* entre les deux
He entered the *competition* without practice.	Il est entré à la *compétition* sans entrainement
What are the rules of the *competition*?	Quelles sont les règles de la *compétition*

789. *condition/état*

His *condition* is very bad.	Son *état* est très mauvais
He suffers from a bad liver *condition*.	Il souffre d'un mauvais *état* du foie
The *condition* of the bus is very bad.	*L'état* du bus est très mauvais

790. *contact/contact*

I have no *contact* with my brother	Je n'ai aucun *contact* avec mon frère
Did you *contact* your sister?	As-tu *contacté* ta sœur ?
Do you have any *contact* number?	As-tu un numéro de *contact* ?

791.*credit/crédit*

The bank will give you some *credit*.	La banque te donnera un *crédit*
The store issued a *credit* note	Le magasin a édité une note de *crédit*
Can I ask for a *credit* of ten dollars?	Puis-je demander un *crédit* de dix dollars ?

792. *currently/actuellement*

Tom is *currently* unemployed	Tom est *actuellement* au chômage
Currently he is our best player	*Actuellement* il est notre meilleur joueur
Tom is *currently* living in Boston	Tom habite *actuellement* à Boston

793. *discuss/discuter*

I need to *discuss* this matter in detail.	Je dois *disctuer* de ce problème en

	détail
What is there to *discuss*?	Qu'y a-t-il à *discuter*
You don't need to *discuss* this	Tu n'as pas besoin de *discuter* ça

794. *distribution/distribution*

The flowers need *distribution.*	Les fleurs ont besoin de *distribution*
Distribution is essential for marketing	La *distribution* est essentielle au marketing
Call her for the prize *distribution.*	Appelle la pour la *distribution* du prix

795. *egg/oeuf*

Would you like an *egg* with the toast?	Voudrais-tu un *œuf* avec le toast ?
How many boiled *eggs* can you eat?	Combien *d'œufs* cuits peux-tu manger ?
I like scrambled *eggs*	J'aime les *œufs* brouillés

796. *entertainment/divertissement*

Music is a form of *entertainment*	La musique est une forme de *divertissement*
There is no *entertainment* in the province	Il n'y a pas de *divertissement* dans la province
There is no *entertainment* for the young	Il n'y a pas de *divertissement* pour les jeunes

797. *final/final*

This decision is *final*	La décision est *finale*
What is the *final* count?	Quel est le décompte *final* ?
I made the *final* decision.	J'ai pris la décision *finale*

798. *happy/heureux*

I am so *happy*	Je suis très *heureux*
I feel *happy* when I see you	Je me sens *heureux* quand je te vois
I feel *happy* every morning	Je me sens *heureux* chaque matin

799. *hope/espère*

I *hope* that he will succeed	*J'espère* qu'il réussira
I *hope* you had a nice trip	*J'espère* que tu auras un bon voyage
Let us *hope* for the best	*Espérons* le meilleur

800. *ice/glace*

The *ice* has melted	La *glace* a fondu
The *ice* is cold	La *glace* est froide
Would you like some *ice*?	Voudrais-tu de la *glace* ?

RANKING: 801–900
The most used words

801. Lift Soulever	802. Mix Mélange	803. Network Réseau	804. North Nord	805. Office Bureau
806. Overall En général	807. Population Population	808. President Président	809. Private Privé	810. Realize Réaliser
811. Responsible Responsable	812. Separate Séparer	813. Square Carré	814. Stop Arrêter	815. Teach Enseigner
816. Unit Unité	817. Western Occidental	818. Yes Oui	819. Alone Seul	820. Attempt Attentat
821. Category Catégorie	822. Cigarette Cigarette	823. Concern Préoccupation	824. Contain Contenir	825. Context Contexte
826. Cute Joli	827. Date Date	828. Effect Effet	829. Extremely Extrêmement	830. Familiar Familier
831. Finally Finalement	832. Fly Voler	833. Follow Suivre	834. Helpful Serviable	835. Introduction Introduction
836. Link Lien	837. Official Officiel	838. Opportunity Opportunité	839. Perfect Parfait	840. Performance Performance
841. Post Publier	842. Recent Récent	843. Refer Référer	844. Solve Résoudre	845. Star Star/Etoile
846. Voice Voix	847. Willing Prêt	848. Born Né	849. Bright Brillant	850. Broad Large
851.	852.	853.	854.	855.

Capital Capitale	Challenge Défi	Comfor Table Confortable	Constantly Constamment	Describe Décrire
856. Despite Malgré	857. Driver Conducteur	858. Flat Plat	859. Flight Vol	860. Friend Ami
861. Gain Acquérir	862. Him Lui	863. Length Longueur	864. Magazine Revue	865. Maybe Peut-Etre
866. Newspaper Journal	867. Nice Joli	868. Prefer Préférer	869. Prevent Prévenir	870. Properly Correctement
871. Relationship Relation	872. Rich Riche	873. Save Sauver	874. Self Auto	875. Shot Tire
876. Soon Bientôt	877. Specifically Spécifiquement	878. Stand Se tenir	879. Teaching Enseignement	880. Warm Chaud
881. Wonderful Génial	882. Young Jeune	883. Ahead Droit	884. Brush Brosse	885. Cell Cellule
886. Couple Couple	887. Daily Quotidien	888. Dealer Revendeur	889. Debate Débat	890. Discover Découvrir
891. Ensure Assurer	892. Exit Sortir	893. Expect Attendre	894. Experienced Expérimenté	895. Fail Achouer
896. Finding Découverte	897. Front Face	898. Function Fonction	899. Heavy Lourd	900. Hello Salut

801. *lift/soulever-monter*

Do you need to *lift* the box?	Tu as besoin de *soulever* la boite?

Can you *lift* to the mountain peak?	Tu peux *monter* au sommet de la montagne?
She tried to *lift* the box	Elle a essayé de *soulever* la boite

802. *mix/mélange*

There has been a *mix* between foreigners	Il y a eu un *mélange* entre les étrangers
Oil and water do not *mix.*	L'huile et l'eau ne se *mélange* pas.
You cannot *mix* meat and milk	Tu ne peux pas *mélanger* viande et lait

803. *network/réseau*

She has a strong *network* of friends.	Elle a un *réseau* d'amis solide.
The police have built a *network*	La police a construit un *réseau*
The communication *network* has broken	Le *réseau* de communication est coupé

804. *north/nord*

The house is located in the *north* side	La maison se situe au *nord* .
Have you been to *North* America?	As tu étais au *nord* de l'Amérique?
Which way is the *North* Pole?	Quelle est le chemin du Pole *Nord*?

805. *office/bureau*

Call me at the *office.*	Appel moi au *bureau.*
Where is the post *office*?	Où se trouve le *bureau* de la poste?
I easily found his *office.*	J'ai trouvé son *bureau* facilement.

806. *overall/en général*

The *overall* system is ruined	*En général* tout le systéme est ruiné
Do you have an idea about the *overall* cost?	As tu une idée *en général* de ce que ça coûte?
What would be the *overall* expenditure?	De combien sera la dépense *en général*?

807. *population/population*

The *population* of China is very large	La *population en Chine est très grande*
The world´s *population* is about 6 billion.	La *population* du monde fait un peu près 6 billion.
The *population* of India is increasing	La *population* en Inde augmente.

808. *president/président*

The *President* travels too much	Le *président* voyage beaucoup
In USA everyone can become *President*	Aux Etats-Unis tout le monde peut devenir *président*
The *President* started the meeting	Le *président* a commencé la réunion.

809.*private/privé-secret*

Can we talk in *private*?	Peut-on parler en *privé*?
Let us keep this *private*	Gardons ça *secret*
Tom has a *private* yacht	Tom a un yacht *privé*

810. *realize/se rendre compte*

Jim failed to *realize* the situation	Jim ne s'est pas *rendu compte* de la situation
He needs to *realize* his mistakes	Il doit *se rendre compte* de ses erreurs
Did you *realize* what you did?	Te *rends tu compte* de ce que tu as fais?

811. *responsible/responsable*

Are you *responsible* for this mess?	Es tu le *responsable* de ce bazar?
I am not *responsible* for what Tom did	Je ne suis pas *responsable* de ce que Tom a fait
Parents are *responsible* for their children	Les parents sont *responsbales* de leur enfants

812. *separate/ séparer*

We got *separated*	Nous nous sommes *séparés*
Tom and I are *separated*	Tom et moi sommes *séparés*
No one can *separate* them	Personne ne peut les *séparer*

813. *square/carré*

A *square* has four sides	Un *carré* a quatres cotés
The *square* root of nine is three	La racine *carré* du neuf est trois
A *square* is always a rectangle	Un *carré* est toujours un rectangulaire

814. *stop/arrêter*

Let us *stop* here	*Arrêtons* nous ici
Nobody can *stop* me	Personne ne peut *m'arrêter*
Stop joking around	*Arrête* de tourner autour

815. *teach/enseigner*

I will *teach* Anthropology at the University	Je vais *enseigner* l'anthropologie à l'université
I will *teach* you a lesson	Je vais *t'enseigner* une lesson
He will *teach* with patience	Il va *enseigner* avec patience

816. *unit/union-unité*

This is a lovely *unit.*	C'est une belle *union.*
This unidad has four bedrooms	Cette *unité* contient quatres chambres à coucher
What is the *unit* of currency here?	Quelle est *l'unité* de la devise ici?

817. *western/occidental*

Mary loves *western* music	Mary aime la music *occidentale*
Cheryl is a big fan of *western* clothes	Cheryl adore les vêtements *occidentaux*
The *western* world is growing slowly	Le monde *occidental* s'aggrandit doucement

818. *yes/oui*

He will not say *yes*	Il ne va pas dire *oui*

I will never say *yes* to her proposal	Je ne vais jamais dire *oui* à leur proposition
Please answer *yes* or no	S'il te plait répond par *oui* ou non

819. *alone/seul*

He was *alone.*	Il était *seul.*
She came *alone.*	Elle est venue *seule.*
Leave my car *alone.*	Laisse ma voiture *seule.*

820.*attempt/tentative-tenter*

There was an *attempt* to break free	Il y avait une *tentative* de fuite
I will never *attempt* this exam	Je ne vais jamais *tenter* cet examen
Do not *attempt* any stunts here	Ne *tente* pas ces accrobaties ici

821. *category/catégorie*

This does not fit any *category*	Ça ne rentre dans une aucune *catégorie*
Category 5 hurricanes cause damage	La *catégorie* 5 des auragans cause des dommages
These two are not in the same *category*	Ces deux ne rentrent pas dans la même *catégorie*

822. *cigarette/cigarette*

He lit up the *cigarette* very slowly	Il a allumé la *cigarette* tout doucement
Smoking *cigarettes* is unhealthy	Fumer les *cigarettes* n'est pas sain

Do not smoke more than a *cigarette* per day	Ne fume pas plus d'une *cigarette* par jour

823. *concern/préoccupation*

That is not my *concern*	Ça ne me *préoccupe* pas
It is no *concern* of mine	Ce n'est pas ma *préoccupation*
I appreciate your *concern*	J'apprécie ta *préoccupation*

824. *contain/contenir*

The boxes *contain* chocolates	Ces boites *contiennent* du chocolats
What does the bag *contain*?	qu'est ce que *contient* le sac?
The wallet must *contain* important things	Le porte feuille doit *contenir* des choses importantes

825. *context/context*

In another *context* the meaning can change	Dans un autre *contexte* ça signifie autre chose
The plan has a political *context*	Le plan a un *contexte* politique
The same problems but a different *context*	Les mêmes problèmes mais un *contexte* différent

826. *cute/joli*

She is really *cute*	Elle est vraiment *jolie*
You have *cute* eyes	Tu as de *jolis* yeux

The couple looks very *cute*	Ce couple est trés *joli*

827. *date/date*

This is the *date* of my marriage	C'est la *date* de mon mariage
Please mark this *date* in the calendar	S'il te plaît marque cette *date* sur le calendrier
First decide on the *date* of journey	Décide d'abord de la *date* du voyage

828. *effect/effet*

The perfume had a very strong *effect*	Le parfum a un *effet* fort
The economic policy.will have a great *effect*	La politique économique va avoir un magnifique *effet*
The *effect* has been pretty widespread	*L'effet* a été très répandu

829. *extremely/extrêmement*

I am *extremely* fond of him	Je me retrouve *extrêmement* en lui
She has was *extremely* wrong	Elle a eu *extrêmement* tord
It was an *extremely* easy victory for us	C'était une victoire *extrêmement* facile pour nous

830. *familiar/familier*

The girl seems to be very *familiar*	La fille semble trés *familière*
This is a *familiar* looking neighborhood	Ce voisinage parait *familier*

I am not very *familiar* with the idea	Je ne suis pas très *familier* avec l'idée

831. *finally/finalement*

Finally we reached an agreement	*Finalement* nous avons trouvé un argument
So you *finally* came here!	Alors, *finalement* tu es venu ici!
We are not quarreling *finally*	*Finalement* nous nous querelions pas

832. *fly/voler*

This bird cannot *fly*	Cet oiseau ne peut pas *voler*
He studied the way birds *fly*	Il a étudie la manière du *vol* des oiseaux
He is afraid to *fly* in an airplane.	Il a peur de *voler* en avion

833. *follow/suivre*

Jim vowed to *follow* a diet plan	Jim s'est voué de *suivre* un régime
You must *follow* torders	Tu dois *suivre* les ordres
There is no need to *follow* him now.	Il n'a y pas intêret de le *suivre* maintenant

834. *helpful/serviable-utile*

Jim has a *helpful* attitude	Jim a une attitude *serviable*
I am not very *helpful* in homicide cases	Je ne suis pas trop *utile* dans les cas criminels
Mary is very *helpful* towards the poor	Maria est très *serviable* envers les pauvres

835. *introduction/introduction*

The businessman needs no *introduction*	L'homme d'affaire n'a pas besoin *d'introduction*
I need to be present for the *introduction*	Je dois être présent pour *l'introduction*
He slept through the *introduction* class	Il a dormi pendant le cours *d'introduction*

836. *link/lien*

There is no *link* between the two brothers	Il n'y a pas de *lien* entre les deux frères
You need to establish a *link*	Tu dois établir un *lien*
I don't find any *link* to the past	Je ne trouve aucun *lien* au passé

837. *official/officiel*

This is *officia*l	C'est *officiel*
It is *official* business	C'est une affaire *officielle*
This makes it *official*	Ça le rend *officiel*

838. *opportunity/opportunité*

I am looking forward to the *opportunity.*	J'attend avec intérêt *l'opportunité*
Do not let such an *opportunity* go by.	Ne laisse pas une telle *opportunité* passer
I will see him at first *opportunity.*	Je le verrai à la première *opportunité*

839. *perfect/parfait*

You seem *perfect.*	Tu semble *parfait*
It was not *perfect.*	Ce n'était pas pas *parfait*
That is so *perfect.*	C'est très *parfait*

840. *performance/performance*

I am pleased with her *performance*	Je suis content de sa *performance*
Tom did not clap Mary's *performance*	Tom n'a pas applaudi la *performance* de Mary
Tom is very pleased with my *performance*	Tom est très content de ma *performance*

841. *post/publier*

I will *post* the letter today.	Je *publierai* la lettre aujourd'hui
Did you *post* anything on the social media?	As-tu *publié* quelque chose dans les médias sociaux ?
How did you forget to *post* the news?	Comment as-tu oublié de *publier* les infos ?

842. *recent/récent*

I have not seen him in *recent* times	Je ne l'ai pas vu dans le temps *récent*
There has been no *recent* development.	Il n'y a pas eu de développement *récent*
I have not seen her *recent* interviews.	Je n'ai pas vu ses entretiens *récents*

843. *refer/référer*

I will *refer* the matter to the authorities	Je *référerai* le probleme aux authorités

Refer to this document each time	*Réfère* toi à ce document chaque fois
Did you *refer* my findings?	As-tu *référé* mes découvertes ?

844. *solve/résoudre*

Jack took his time to *solve* this case	Jack a pris son temps pour *résoudre* ce cas
Did you *solve* the equations?	As tu *résolu* l'équation?
I have to *solve* the numerical problems	Je dois *résoudre* le probléme numérique

845. *star/star-étoile*

She made me a *star.*	Elle a fait de moi une *star.*
Who is your favorite TV *star*?	C'est qui ta *star* de télé préférée?
Have you ever seen a shooting *star*?	As tu jamais vu une *étoile* filante?

846. *voice/voix*

She raised her *voice.*	Elle a haussé sa *voix.*
Tony's *voice* is nice.	La *voix* de tony est belle.
I am happy to hear your *voice.*	Je suis content d'entendre ta *voix.*

847. *willing/prêt*

I *willing to* give you a loan	Je suis prêt à te donner un *prêt*
The woman was willing to divorce	La femme était *prête* pour le divorce
Are you *willing to* invite your mother?	Es tu *prêt* à inviter ta mère?

848. *born/naitre*

When was she *born*?	Où est ce qu'elle est *née*?
Where was Tom *born*?	Où Tom est il *né*?
He was *born* in Ohio.	Il est *né* à Ohio.

849. *bright/brillant*

That is a *bright* idea.	C'est une idée *brillante.*
He is by no means *bright.*	Il n'est en aucun manière *brillant.*
The light from the lamp is very *bright.*	La lumière de la lampe est très *brillante.*

850. *broad/large-ouverte*

The street is very *broad*	Le boulevard est très *large*
Mary is a *broad*-minded woman	Mary est une femme *ouverte* d'esprit
He shot the boy in a *broad* alley	Il a tiré sur le garçon dans une *large* allée

851. *capital/capitale-capital*

The *capita*l of Italy is Rome	La *capitale* de l'Italie est Rome
London is one of the busiest *capital* cities	Londre est l'une des villes *capitales* les plus fréquentées
Could you raise the required *capital*?	Pourrais-tu réunir le *capital* requis?

852. *challenge/défi*

This is the biggest *challenge* in my life.	C'est le grand *défi* dans ma vie.
It is a tough *challenge* for me.	C'est un *défi* difficile pour moi.
Do not *challenge* him to a fight.	Ne le mets pas au *défi* de se combattre.

853. *comfortable/confortable*

Tom seems quite *comfortable*	Tom semble assez *confortable*
I am very *comfortable*	Je suis très *confortable*
I know you are not *comfortable*	Je sais que tu n'es pas *confortable*

854. *constantly/constamment*

His wife nags him *constantly.*	Sa femme le critique *constamment.*
Tom and Mary fight *constantly.*	Tom et Mary se disputent *constamment.*
She is *constantly* writing letters.	Elle écrit *costamment* des lettres.

855. *describe/décrire*

I will try to *describe* the place	Je vais essayer de *décrire* la place
Let me *describe* the situation	Laisse moi *décrire* la situation
Can you *describe* the crime scene?	Peux tu *décrire* la scéne de crime?

856. *despite/malgré*

I love him *despite* his faults	Je l'aime *malgré* ces défauts
Despite all his wealth, he is stingy	*Malgré* sa richesse, il est avare

We push ahead *despite* everything	On est allé de l'avant *malgré* tout

857. *driver/conductrice-conducteur*

Is she a taxi *driver*?	Est ce qu'elle est *conductrice* de taxi?
Do not be a back seat *driver*	Ne sois pas un *conducteur* du siége arrière
The *driver* told us which bus we should take	Le *conducteur* nous a dit quell bus prendre

858. *flat/plat*

I got a *flat* tire.	J'ai eu un pneu à *plat.*
My cycle has a *flat* tire.	Ma vélo a un pneu à *plat.*
I love *flat* breads.	J'aime le pain *plat.*

859. *flight/vol*

Did you miss the *flight*?	As tu raté le *vol*?
What time does your *flight* take-off?	À quelle heure ton *vol* décolle?
My *flight* is on schedule.	Mon *vol* est sur le calendrier.

860. *friend/ami*

A *friend* in need is a friend indeed	C'est dans le besoin qu'on reconnait ses vrais *amis*
Your *friend* looks pretty handsome.	Ton *ami* est très joli.
I can count on my *friend*	Je ne peux pas compter sur mon *ami*

861. *gain/acquérir*

Tom must *gain* a little bit of weight	Tom doit *acquérir* un peu du poid
She began to *gain* weight	Elle a commencé à *acquérir* du poid
Tom needs to *gain* more knowledge.	To a besoin *d'acquérir* plus de connaissance

862. *him/lui-l'*

I am in love with *him*	Je suis amoureuse de *lui*
I can count on *him* whenever necessary.	je ne peux pas compter sur *lui* à chaque fois que nécessaire
I really don't like him	Vraiment je ne *l'*aime pas

863. *length/longueur*

What is the *length* of this courtyard?	Quelle est la *longueur* de cette cour?
I would like to know the *length* of this bed	Je veux bien savoir la *longueur* de ce lit
The *length* of the field is 1000 yards	La *longueur* de ce terrain est de 1000 yards

864. *magazine/revue*

I have subscribed to this *magazine.*	J'ai souscris à cette *revue.*
Can you buy that *magazine* for me?	Peux-tu m'acheter cette *revue*?
It is an old *magazine.*	C'est une ancienne *revue.*

865. *maybe/peut-être*

Maybe he won't become famous.	*Peut-être* il veut de venir célèbre.
Maybe you would better come with us.	C'est mieux *peut-être* que tu viennes avec nous.
Maybe he has lots of girlfriends.	*Peut-être* qu'il a beaucoup de copines.

866. *newspaper/journal*

This *newspaper* is free	Ce *journal* est gratuit.
He was reading a *newspaper*	Il lisait un *journal.*
I read about him in the *newspaper*	J'ai lu à propos de lui dans un *journal.*

867. *nice/bonne*

He is *nice.*	Il est *bon.*
Have a *nice* day.	Passez une *bonne* journée.
It is a *nice* day.	C'est une *bonne* journée.

868. *prefer/préfèrer*

I *prefer* reading to writing	Je *préfère* la lecture à l'écriture
I *prefer* to travel by air	Je *préfère* voyager par avion
Which wine do you *prefer*	Quel vin *préfère*–tu ?

869. *prevent/empêcher*

The driver could not *prevent* the accident	Le conducteur n'a pas pu *empêcher* l'accident

I could not *prevent* him from leaving	Je n'ai pas pu l'*empêcher* de partir
We cannot *prevent* Jim from seeing Cheryl.	On ne peut pas *empêcher* Jim de voir Cheryl.

870. *properly/ correctement*

You must write *properly*	Tu doit écrire *correctement*
Tom must drive *properly*	Tom doit conduire *correctement*
Properly arrange the books	Organise *correctement* les livres

871. *relationship/relation*

I am in a *relationship*	Je suis dans une *relation*
They want to renew their *relationship*	Ils ne veulent pas renouer leur *relation*
Are you in a *relationship*?	Es-tu dans une *relation ?*

872. *rich/riche-richesse*

Rockefeller is a *rich* man	Rockefeller est un homme *riche*
USA is *rich* in natural resources	USA est *riche* en ressources naturelles
From rags to *riches*	De la misère à la *richesse*

873. *save/sauver-protége*

God *save* the Queen	Que Dieu *protége* la reine
The bodyguard *saved* his life	Le garde a *sauvé* sa vie

She risked her life to *save* him	Elle a risqué sa vie pour le *sauver*

874. *self/auto*

I will paint a *self*-portrait	Je vais peindre *mon auto*-portrait
He had a kind of *self* realization	Il a une sorte d'*auto*-réalisation
This camera works on a *self* timer	Cette caméra a un minuteur *auto*matique

875. *shot/tire*

The farmer *shot* the injured horse	Le fermier *tire* sur le cheval blessé
The young boy *shot* accidentally	Le petit garçon, lui a *tiré* accidentellement
An unknown assassin *shot* the king	Un assassin inconnu *tire* sur le roi

876. *soon/bientôt-Quand*

I will deliver the letter *soon*	Je vais délivrer la lettre *bientôt*
How *soon* can you come?	*Quand* est-ce-que tu vas venir ?
The train will reach very *soon*	Le train va arriver très *bientôt*

877. *specifically/spécifiquement*

I would like *specifically* this information	Je veux *spécifiquement* cette information
She *specifically* stated she would come	Elle a déclaré *spécifiquement* qu'elle a

	va venir
My doctor told me *specifically* to avoid meat.	Mon docteur m'a dit *spécifiquement* d'éviter la viande

878. *stand/se tenir-arrêt*

The book *stands* on the table	Le livre *se tient* sur la table
Where is the bus *stand* located?	Où se trouve *l'arrêt* du bus ?
Can you *stand* on one leg?	Pouvez –vous vous *tenir* sur une jambe ?

879. *teaching/enseigner-enseignement*

I am *teaching* in the University	J'*enseigne* dans une université
What do you do apart from *teaching*?	Que-est-ce tu fais mis-à-part l'*enseignement* ?
Teaching is a noble profession.	L'*enseignement* est une noble profession

880. *warm/chaud*

The room was *warm*	La chambre est *chaude*
The winter is *warm*	L'hiver est *chaud*
This sweater is *warm*	Ce tricot est *chaud*

881. *wonderful/formidable*

We had a *wonderful* time	Nous avons eu un *formidable* moment
She is a *wonderful* woman	C'est une femme *formidable*
She gave me a *wonderful* present	Elle m'a donné un *formidable* cadeau

882. *young/jeune*

I am *young.*	Je suis *jeune.*
He looks *young.*	Il paraît *jeune.*
Being *young* is better than being old	Etre *jeune* est mieux qu'être vieux

883. *ahead/devant-droit*

The car went *ahead* of us	La voiture marchait *devant* nous
Jim moved *ahead* in his career	Jim avance *droit* dans sa carrière
Ahead you will find the spot	tu vas trouver l'endroit *devant*

884. *brush/brosse*

She gave him the *brush*	Elle lui a donné la *brosse*
Brush your teeth after each meal	*Brossez* vos dents après chaque repas
She cleaned the kitchen floor with a *brush*	Elle a nettoyé le sol de la cuisine avec la *brosse*

885. *cell/cellule/pile*

The prison *cell* is very hot	La *cellule* du prison est très haute

You can use a dry *cell* in this machine	Vous pouvez utiliser des *piles* séches pour cette machine
Where is the *cell* of Goering?	Où sont les *cellules* de Goering ?

886. *couple/couple*

We are a married *couple*	Nous sommes un *couple* marié
I am taking a *couple* of days off	Je prends un *couple* de jours de repos
May I ask you a *couple* of questions?	Puis-je vous demander un *couple* de questions ?

887. *daily/quotidien-quotidiennement*

This is a *daily* newspaper	C'est un journal *quotidien*
I always listen to the *daily* news	J'écoute toujours les infos *quotidiennes*
I drink a glass of milk on a *daily* basis	Je bois un verre de lait *quotidiennement*

888. *dealer/revendeur*

The *dealer* is very dishonest	Le *revendeur* est tès malhonnête
The drug *dealer* was very shrewd	Le *revendeur* de la droge était très malin
Contact the *dealer*	contacte le *revendeur*

889. *debate/débat/débattre*

There is a *debate* about capital	Il y a un *débat* sur la peine capital

punishment	
The long *debate* ended in a stalemate	Le long *débat* s'est términé par une impasse
It is better to *debate* the question	C'est mieux de *débattre* la question

890. *discover/découvrir*

He was lucky to *discover* oil	Il était chanceux de *découvrir* le pétrol
We have yet to *discover* the solution	Nous n'avons pas encore *découvert* la solution
Studying you can *discover* your ignorance	Etudiez vous pouvez *découvrir* votre ignorance

891. *ensure/assurer*

Careful preparations will *ensure* success.	Les préparations minutieuses *assureront* la réussite
You need to *ensure* his presence.	Tu dois *assurer* sa présence
Did you *ensure* he got the documents?	Es-tu *assuré* qu'il a les documents ?

892. *exit/sortir*

The *exit* is on the other side	La *sortie* est de l'autre coté
The *exit* gate is on the left	La *sortie* porte de est sur la gauche
You should *exit* the museum now.	Vous devez *sortir* de la musée maintenant

893. *expect/attendre*

I do not *expect* anything from you	Je n'*attends* rien venant de vous
Did you *expect* this?	*Attendais*-tu cela?
Tom will *expect* a gift on her birthday	Tom *attendra* un cadeau pour son anniversaire

894. *experienced/experimenté*

Jim is an *experienced* plumber	Jim est un plumbier *experimenté*
I am *experienced* engineer	Je suis un ingénieur *experimenté*
Always rely on *experience*	Comptez toujours sur l'*experience*

895. *fail/ échouer*

I will *fail* in all projects	Je vais *échouer* dans tous les projets
Jim will *fail* in physics.	Jim va *échouer* en physique.
Tom's project will *fail* .	Le projet de Jim va *échouer*.

896. *finding/découverte*

The *finding* is not very clear.	La *découverte* n'est pas tès clair.
Can you give details about your *finding*?	Pouve-vous donner plus de détails à propos de ta *découverte*?
Findings are never an easy task	Les *découvertes* ne sont jamais chose facile

897. *front/devant*

The *front* door is locked	La porte de dev*ant* est verrouillée.
The *front* gallery is beautiful	La la gallerie de *devant* est jolie
Lock the *front* door when you leave	Regarde la porte de *devant* quand tu pars

898. *function/fonction*

The *function* of language is to communicate	La *fonction* de la langue est la communication
This body *function* is essential	La *fonction* de ce corps est essentielle
This software has many *functions.*	Ce logiciel a plusieurs *fonctions*

899. *heavy/lourd*

The luggage is very *heavy*	Ce bagage est très *lourd*
The boy is now very *heavy*	Le garçon est maintenant très *lourd*
The bag is too *heavy* to carry	Le sac est trop *lourd* pour carry

900. *hello/bonjour*

Did you say *hello* to her?	Lui as-tu dit *salut ?*
Hello! How are you?	*Salut* ! comment vas-tu ?
I must say *hello* to him	Je dois lui dire *salut*

RANKING: 901–1000
The most used words

901. Highly Très	902. Immediately Immédiatement	903. Impossible Impossible	904. Invest Investir	905. Lack Manque
906. Lake Lac	907. Lead Diriger	908. Listen Ecouter	909. Living Vivant	910. Member Membre
911. Message Message	912. Phone Téléphone	913. Plant Plante	914. Plastic Plastic	915. Reduce Réduire
916. Relatively Relativement	917. Scene Scène	918. Serious Sérieux	919. Slowly Lentement	920. Speak Parler
921. Spot Place	922. Summer Eté	923. Taste Goût	924. Theme Thème	925. Towards Vers
926. Track Piste	927. Valuable Précieux	928. Whatever Ce que	929. Wing Aile	930. Worry Inquiet
931. Appear Apparaitre	932. Appearance Apparence	933. Association Association	934. Brain Cerveau	935. Button Bouton
936. Click Clique	937. Concept Concept	938. Correct Correct	939. Customer Client	940. Death Mort
941. Desire Désir	942. Discussion Discussion	943. Explain Expliquer	944. Explore Explorer	945. Express Rapide
946. Fairly Justement	947. Fixed Reglé	948. Foot Pied	949. Gas Gaz	950. Handle Controle
951.	952.	953.	954.	955.

Housing Logement	Huge Grand	Inflation Inflation	Influence Influence	Insurance Assurance
956. Involve Impliquer	957. Leading Dirige	958. Lose Perdre	959. Meet Rencontrer	960. Mood Humeur
961. Notice Remarquer	962. Primarily Principalement	963. Rain Pluie	964. Rare Rare	965. Release Libérer
966. Sell Vendre	967. Slow Lent	968. Technical Technique	969. Typical Typique	970. Upon Sur
971. Wall Mur	972. Woman Femme	973. Advice Conseil	974. Afford Permettre	975. Agree Accord
976. Base Base	977. Blood Sang	978. Clean Nettoyer	979. Competitive Compétitif	980. Completely Complétement
981. Critical Critique	982. Damage Dommage	983. Distance Distance	984. Effort Effort	985. Electronic Electronique
986. Expression Expression	987. Feeling Sentiment	988. Finish Finir	989. Fresh Frais	990. Hear Entendre
991. Immediate Immédiat	992. Importance Importance	993. Normal Normal	994. Opinion Opinion	995. Otherwise Autrement
996. Pair Paire	997. Payment Paiement	998. Plus Plus	999. Press Presse/Appuyer	1000. Reality Réalité

901. *highly/très*

You are a *highly* efficient manager	Tu es un gérant *très* efficace

Your tips have been proven *highly* effective	Il a été prouvé que tes conseils sont *très* efficaces
This con man is *highly* well known	Cet homme est *très* bien connu

902. *immediately/immédiatement*

My dad must be admitted *immediately*	Mon père doit etre admis *immédiatement*
She recognized him *immediately.*	Elle l'a reconnu *immédiatement*
She *immediately* quit the job	Elle a *immédiatement* quitté le travail

903. *impossible/impossible*

What you suggested is almost *impossible*	Ce que t'as suggeré est presque *impossible*
Nothing is *impossible* in this world	Rien n'est *impossible* dans ce monde
Never think that a job is *impossible*	Ne penses jamais qu'un travail est *impossible*

904. *invest/investir*

I would love to *invest* in mutual funds	J'aimerais bien *investir* dans des fonds mutuels
He promised he will *invest* a lot of money	Il a promis qu'il va *investir* beaucoup d'argent
Do not *invest* a huge capital at once	*N'investis* pas un énorme fond à la fois

905. *lack/manque*

He failed due to *lack* of money	Il a échoué à cause du *manque* d'argent
His *lack* of technical knowledge harmed him	Son *manque* de connaissance technique l'a nouié
This *lack* of common sense is very common	Ce *manque* de bon sens est très répandu

906. *lake/lac*

The house by the *lake* looks beautiful	Cette maison près du *lac* est jolie
One day I will purchase a condo in the *lake*	Un jour je vais acheter un appartement au *lac*
Is allowed boating on this l*ake*?	Est ce que la navigation est permise dans ce *lac*?

907. *lead/dirige*

Lead your people and they will be grateful	*Dirige* tes gens et ils seront reconnaissants
Just follow my *leadership*	Juste suis ma *direction*
Tom *leads* with examples	Tom *dirige* avec des exemples

908. *listen/écouter*

She doesn't *listen* to him	Elle ne *l'écoutes* pas
Nobody would *listen* to me	Personne ne voudra *m'écouter*
Don't *listen* to her	Ne *l'écoutes* pas

909. *living/vivant-vie*

He is a *living* example of a true magician	Il est un exemple *vivant* d'un vrai magicien
I can earn my *living* running the shop	Je peux gagner ma *vie* par travailler dans la boutique
What do you do for a *living*?	Qu'est ce que tu fais pour gagner ta *vie*?

910. *member/membre*

Are you a *member* of that society?	T'es un *membre* de cette societé?
I wish to be a library *member*	Je veux etre un *membre* de la librairie
What are the rules of a new *member*?	Quelles sont les règles d'un nouveau *membre*?

911. *message/message*

Please send him this *message*	S'il te plait envoies lui ce *message*
Can I leave a *message*?	Est ce que je peux laisser un *message*?
Leave me a *message*, please.	Laisses moi un *message*, s'il te plait.

912. *phone/téléphone*

I need to buy a new *phone*	J'ai besoin d'acheter un nouveau *téléphone*
Did you get the latest model of the *phone*?	Tu as eu le dernier model du *téléphone*?
It is hard to survive without a cell	Il est difficile de survivre sans un

phone.	*téléphone* portable

913. *plant/plante*

The terrorists will *plant* a bomb.	Les terroristes vont *planter* une bombe
I asked the gardener to *plan*t some trees	Jai demandé au gardien de *planter* quelques arbres
Water please the *plants*	Arrose les *plantes* s'il te plait

914. *plastic/plastique*

Do you accept *plastic*?	Tu acceptes le *plastique*?
Tom is a *plastic* surgeon	Tom est un chirurgien *plastique*
Plastic does not burn easily	Le *plastique* ne brule pas facilement

915. *reduce/réduire*

The world must *reduce* carbon in the air	Le monde doit *réduire* le carbon dans l'air
I need to *reduce* my weight	Je dois *réduire* mon poids
Did you *reduce* your alcohol intake?	Tu as *réduis* ton apport d'alcool?

916. *relatively/relativement*

She speaks *relatively* fast	Elle parle *relativement* rapidement
She speaks *relatively* quick	Elle parle *relativement* vite

The store was *relatively* empty	Le magasin était *relativement* vide

917. *scene/scène*

A crowd gathered at the *scene*	Une foule s'est réunie à la *scène*
They went to the *scene* of the accident	Ils sont partis à la *scène* de l'accident
The last *scene* was very emotional	La dernière *scène* était très émotionnelle

918. *serious/sérieux*

Mary is not at all *serious* about her studies	Mary n'est pas du tout *sérieuse* à propos de ses études
Are you *serious* on this issue?	Tu es *sérieux* sur ce problème?
I need to be *serious* on this matter.	Je dois etre *sérieux* sur cette affaire

919. *slowly/lentement*

My mother speaks *slowly*	Ma mère parle *lentement*
I opened the door *slowly*	J'ai ouvert la porte *lentement*
Please speak more *slowly*	S'il te plait parle plus *lentement*

920. *speak/parler*

Speak out and you will be heard.	*parle* et tu seras entendu
Did you *speak* to Tom about this?	As-tu *parlé* à Tom à propos de ça?
I need to *speak* to your parents	Je dois *parler* à tes parents

921. *spot/place*

I was in the real *spot*	J'étais à la vraie *place*
The referee pointed to the penalty *spot.*	L'arbitre a fait signe pour la *place* de pénalité
He is an expert in selecting *spots*	Il est un expert pour selecter les *places*

922. *summer/été*

It has been a long *summer* for the coach	Il a été un long *été* pour l'entraineur
The *summer* months were very hot	Les mois *d'été* étaient très chauds
I will go to London in the *summer* vacation	Je vais partir à Londres dans les vacances *d'été*

923. *taste/goût*

This fruit does not *taste* good	Ce fruit n'a pas un bon *gout*
I don't like your *taste* regarding colors	Je n'aime pas ton *gout* concernant les couleurs
The *taste* of the chicken dish is delicious	Le *gout* du plat de poulet est délicieux

924. *theme/thème*

This year the festival is based on a *theme*	Cette année le festival est basé sur un *thème*

Did you listen to the movie's *theme* song	As-tu écouté la chanson *thème* du film
The *theme* of the conference is superb	Le *thème* de la conférence est superbe

925. *towards/vers*

He walked *towards* the man with resolution	Il a marché *vers* l'homme avec résolution
The batsman walked *towards* the pavilion	Le batteur a marché *vers* le pavillon
I ran *towards* the bus stand	Je crous *vers* l'arrêt du bus

926. *track/piste*

I got confused about the *track*	Je suis confus à propos de la *piste*
We are on the right *track*	Nous sommes sur la bonne *piste*
I have selected the wrong *track*	J'ai sélectionné la mauvaise *piste*

927. *valuable/précieux*

I learned a *valuable* lesson today	J'ai appris une leçon *précieuse* aujourd'hui
We are wasting *valuable* time here	Nous perdons un temps *précieux* ici
Tom has found something *valuable*	Tom a trouvé quelque chose de *précieux*

928.*whatever/ce que-n'importe quel*

Do *whatever* you like.	Fais *ce que* tu aimes.
Do *whatever* he tells you.	Fais *ce qu*'il te dit
Eat *whatever* food you like.	Manges *n'importe quel* aliment tu aimes

929. *wing/aile*

I approached the left *wing*	J'ai approché *l'aile* gauche
Birds need wings to fly	Les oiseaux ont besoin *d'ailes* pour voler
The bird had a broken *wing*	L'oiseau a une *aile* cassé

930. *worry/inquiète*

Do not *worry* about it	Ne *t'inquiète* pas pour ça
She told him not to *worry*.	Elle lui a dit de ne pas *s'inquiéter*
Do not *worry* about the past.	Ne *t'inquiète* pas à propos du passé

931. *appear/apparaitre*

They *appeared* dead	Ils sont *apparus* morts
She failed to *appear* in court	Elle a échoué de *paraitre* au tribunal
Tom and Mary *appeared* suddenly	Tom et Mary sont *apparus* soudainement

932. Appearance/apparence

Appearance is very important in life	*L'apparence* est très importante dans la vie
Don't be fooled by her *appearance*	Ne sois pas dupé par son *apparence*
Do not judge a man by his *appearance*	Ne juges pas un homme par son *apparence*

933. Association/association

They have formed a nationwide *association*	Ils ont formés une *association* à l'échelle nationale
This kind of *association* should be banned	Ce genre *d'associations* doit etre bannis
The *association* has passed a prohibition	*L'association* a réussis une interdiction

934. Brain/cerveau-neuro

He has a good *brain*	Il a un bon *cerveau*
Tom had a *brain* tumor	Tom a une tumeur de *cerveau*
He is an excellent *brain* surgeon	Il est un excellent *neuro*-chirurgien

935. Button/bouton

This *button* is loose	Ce *bouton* est en vrac
You only have to push the red *button*	Tu dois seulement appuyer sur le *bouton* rouge
Please *sew* the *button* for me.	S'il te plait couds le *bouton* pour moi.

936. Click/clique

Just *click* on some photos of the couple	Juste *cliques* sur quelques photos du couple
We did not *click* in the right link	On a pas *cliqué* sur le bon lien
One more *click* and we are done	Un autre *clique* et on a finit

937. Concept/concept

The *concept* of the festival is unique	Le *concept* du festival est unique
I liked the *concept* of the documentary	J'aimais le *concept* du documentaire
The *concept* of your research is god	Le *concept* de ta recherche est bon

938. Correct/corriger

He must *correct* the spelling in the book	Il doit *corriger* l'orthographe au livre
Can you *correct* your behavior?	Peux-tu *corriger* ton comportement?
I need to *correct* the answers	Je dois *corriger* les réponses

939. Customer/client

The *customer* is frustrated with our service.	Le *client* est frustré de notre service
More data about each *customer* is required	Plus de données à propos de chaque *client* est obligatoire
Please suggest products to the *customer*	Propose s'il te plait des produits au *client*

940. Death/mort

Tom was shocked by the *death* of his friend	Tom a été choqué de la *mort* de son ami
Do you know the cause of this *death*?	Connais-tu la cause de sa *mort*?
What caused his *death*?	Qu'est ce qui a causé sa *mort*?

941. Desire/désir

I have a *desire* to become a pilot	J'ai un *désir* de devenir un pilote
What is your true *desire* in life?	C'est quoi ton vrai *désir* dans la vie?
Do you *desire* to get noticed by the media?	*Désires*-tu être remarqué par les médias?

942. Discussion/discussion

The police chief had a strong discussion	Le chef de police avait une forte *discussion*
I have been called for a *discussion*.	j'ai été appellé pour une *discussion*
The *discussion* on law and order is useful	La *discussion* sur la loi et l'ordre est terrible

943. Explain/expliquer

Please *explain* the situation	S'il te plait *expliques* la situation
I cannot *explain* it very well	Je ne peux pas bien *l'expliquer*

I will *explain* the incident.	Je vais *expliquer* l'incident

944. Explore/explorer

Let us *explore* the possibilities	Laisses nous *explorer* les possibilités
He likes to *explore* underground caves	Il aime *explorer* les caves souterraines
He hopes to *explore* the island	Il souhaite *explorer* l'ile

945. Express/exprimer

I will *express* my feeling now	Je vais *exprimer* mon sentiment maintenant
Tom had an chance to express himself	Tom avait une chance de *s'exprimer*
I did not *express* any interest in her business.	Je n'ai *exprimé* aucun intérêt dans son entreprise

946. Fair/juste

The students had a *fair* chance	Les étudiants avaient une *juste* chance
I am *fair to everybody.*	Je suis *juste* avec tout le monde
It is a *fair* deal for the school	C'est un échange *juste* pour l'école

947. Fixed/réglé

I have *fixed* the problem on my own.	J'ai *réglé* le problème seul
The plumber *fixed* the leaking pipe.	Le plombier a *réglé* la fuite du tuyeau
Can this error be *fixed*?	Cette erreur peut-elle se *régler*?

948. Foot/pied

We traveled on *foot.*	On a voyagé à *pieds.*
Do you go to school on *foot*?	Tu pars à l'école à *pieds*?
He hurt his left *foot* when he fell.	Il a blessé son *pied* gauche quand il est tombé.

949. Gas/gaz

Turn off the *gas*	Eteins le *gaz*
This heater burns *gas*	Ce réchauffeur brule du *gaz*
Where do I pay for the *gas*?	Ou est-ce que je paye pour le *gaz*?

950. Handle/controler

The handling of the situation was wrong	Le *controle* de la situation était faux
Can you *handle* this situation?	Peux-tu *controler* cette situation?
She handled the anger carefully	Elle a *controlé* sa colère avec attention

951. Housing/ logement

Construction for the new *housing* is going on	La construction du nouveau *logement* est en cours
This old building is our *housing*	Cet ancien immeuble est notre *logement*

The *housing* board met already	Le conseil de *logement* s'est déjà réuni

952. Huge/énorme

I received a *huge* fortune.	J'ai reçu une *énorme* fortune
My surprise was huge	Ma surprise était *énorme*
He is a *huge* man, tall and strong	Il est un homme *énorme*, grand et fort

953. Inflation/inflation

The country is under a high *inflation* rate	Ce pays est sous un taux élevé *d'inflation*
We need to curb *inflation*	On a besoin de freiner *l'inflation*
What is the rate of *inflation* in Europe?	Quel est le taux de *l'inflation* en europe?

954. Influence/influence

Tom is a bad *influence*	Tom est une mauvaise *influence*
You are a bad *influence.*	Tu es une mauvaise *influence.*
TV has a bad *influence* on children.	La télévision a une mauvaise *influence* sur les enfants.

955. insurance/*assurance*

You must buy a car *insurance*	Tu dois acheter une *assurance* de voiture

Is this the best health *insurance* plan?	Est-ce que c'est le meilleur plan *d'assurance* sur la santé?
I am going to compare the *insurance* policies	Je vais comparer les politiques des *assurances*

956. *involve/impliquer*

I did not mean to *involve* you.	J'ai pas eu l'intention de *t'impliquer.*
This *involves* the whole community	ça *implique* toute la communauté
What does this decision *involve*?	Cette décision *implique* quoi?

957.*leading/Diriger*

Tom is *leading* the party.	Tom *dirige* la fete.
Are you *leading* this change?	Est-ce que tu *dirige* ce changement?
Are you l*eading* the camp group?	Est-ce que tu *dirige* le groupe de camping

958.*lose/perdre*

Do not *lose* your attitude	Ne *perds* pas ton attitude
Do not *lose* your temper	Ne *perds* pas ton sang-froid
Do not *lose* your sleep over that	Ne *perds* pas ton sommeil à cause de ça

959. *meet/rencontrer*

Nice to *meet* you	Ravie de te *rencontrer*
Whom did you *meet*?	Qui t'as *rencontré*?
Where will we *meet*?	Ou va t-on se *rencontrer*?

960. *mood/humeur*

She was in the *mood* for a walk	Elle était *d'humeur* à marcher
She was not in the *mood* for lunch	Elle n'était pas *d'humeur* à manger le déjeuner
I am in *mood* for a few drinks	Je suis *d'humeur* à boire qualques boissons

961. *notice/remarquer*

Did you *notice* any change?	As-tu *remarqué* un changement?
Wait until you *notice* a change	Attends jusqu'à ce que tu *remarques* un changement
I did not *notice* the difference	Je n'ai pas *remarqué* la différence

962. *primarily/principalement*

The PC is used *primarily* by my people	Le PC est utilisé *principalement* par mes gens
The norm involves *primarily* the children	La norme implique *principalement* les enfants
Hia values are *primarily* our own	Ses valeurs sont *principalement* les notres

963. *rain/pluie*

It may *rain.*	Il pourrait *pleuvoir.*
It looks like *rain.*	ça ressemble à la *pluie.*
Will it *rain* today?	va t-il *pleuvoir* aujourd'hui?

964. *rare/rare*

I like *rare* cuisine	J'aime la cuisine *rare*
I found a *rare* book I had been looking for.	J'ai trouvé un livre *rare* que j'ai été entrain de chercher
It is not *rare* to find an octogenarian here	Ce n'est pas *rare* de trouver un octogénaire ici

965. *release/libérer*

Tom will be *released* from prison today	Tom sera *libéré* aujourd'hui de la prison
I will *release* all the documents	Je vais *libérér* tout les documents
The Judge asked to *release* the man.	Le juge a demandé de *libérer* l'homme.

966. *sell/vendre*

Her books *sell* pretty well.	Ses livres se *vendent* bien
Will you *sell* your car to me?	Vas-tu me *vendre* ta voiture?
Will you *sell* your this year?	Vas-tu *vendre* ta maison cette année?

967. *slow/lentement*

Just *slow* down	juste vas *lentement*
Tom is going too *slow*	Tom va très *lentement*
We took it *slow*	On l'a pris *lentement*

968. *technical/technique*

She advises him on *technical* matters	Elle le conseille sur des affaires *techniques*
There are some *technical* difficulties	Il y a quelques problèmes *techniques*
They are friends from my *technical* school	Ils sont amis de mon école *technique*

969. *typical/typique*

This is very *typical* of Jim	C'est très *typique* de Jim
It was a *typical* night	C'était une nuit *typique*
He gave the *typical* greeting	Il a donné la salutation *typique*

970. *upon/sur*

I hit *upon* the floor	J'ai frappé *sur* le sol
Fate fell *upon* me.	Le sort est tombé *sur* moi.
You can rest *upon* the bed	Tu peux te reposer *sur* le lit

971. *wall/mur*

This *wall* feels cold	Ce *mur* est froid

Ken jumped over the *wall*	Ken a sauté le *mur*
She painted the *wall* color pink	Elle a peint le *mur* en rose

972. *woman/femme*

She is a quiet *woman*	Elle est une *femme* silencieuse
The *woman* is reading	La *femme* est entrain de lire
Who is that old *woman*?	Qui est cette vielle *femme*?

973. *advice/conseil*

I need *advice.*	J'ai besoin d'un *conseil*
Take my *advice.*	Prends mon *conseil*
Follow my *advice.*	Suis mon *conseil*

974. *afford/ permettre*

Tom cannot *afford* it	Tom ne peut pas se *le permettre*
We cannot *afford* to be choosy	On ne peut pas se *permettre* de choisir
I cannot *afford* anything like that	Je ne peux pas *permettre* quelque chose comme ça

975. *agree/accord*

I *agree* with Tom on that matter	Je suis *d'accord* avec Tom sur cette affaire
I *agree* with you as, as always	Je suis *d'accord* avec toi, comme

	toujours
They might *agree* tomorrow	Ils pourraient etre *d'accord* demain

976. *base/base*

He threw the ball to first *base*	I a la lancé la balle a la première *base*
He did not come back to the *base* yesterday	Il n'est pas revenu à la *base* hier
Tom stole a *base*	Tom a volé une *base*

977. *blood/sang*

I have high *blood* pressure	J'ai une hypertension de *sang*
Have you ever donated *blood*?	As-tu déjà donné du *sang*?
You should go for a *blood* test.	Tu dois faire une analyse de *sang*

978.*clean/nettoyer*

Clean your room.	*Nettoie* ta chambre.
Clean up the room.	*Nettoie* la chambre.
Is the bath *clean*?	Est-ce que la salle de bain est *nettoyée*?

979. *competitive/compétitif*

Tom is very *competitive* in nature	Tom est très *compétitif* de nature
This is a highly *competitive* world	C'est un monde extremement

	compétitif
Do not be too much *competitive*	Ne sois pas trop *compétitif*

980. *completely/complètement*

I trust him *completely*	J'ai *complètement* confiance en lui
I am *completely* exhausted	Je suis *complètement* fatiguée
She ignores him *completely*	Elle l'ignore *complètement*

981. *critical/critique*

Tom had been very *critical* about this	Tom a été très *critique* sur ça
At least he did not look so *critical*	Au moins il n'a pas semblé très *critique*
He is in a very *critical* condition	Il est dans une situation très *critique*

982. *damage/dommage*

The *damage* is done	Le *dommage* est fait
The storm caused a lot of *damage*	L'orage a causé beaucoup de *dommages*
There has been *damages* by the earthquake	Des *dommages* ont été causés par le tremblement de terre

983. *distance/distance*

Keep your *distance*	Gardes ta *distance*

I cannot judge from this *distance*	Je ne peux pas juger de cette *distance*
I saw a town in the *distance*	J'ai vu une ville de cette *distance*

984. *effort/effort*

I wonder if my *effort* will pay off	Je me demande si mon *effort* va payer
He found all his *efforts* useless	Il a trouvé tout ses *efforts* innutiles
We cannot help admiring their *effort*	On peut pas aider à admirer leur *effort*

985. *electronic/électronique*

He is studying *electronic* engineering	Il étudie l'ingénieurie *électronique*
It is an *electronic* car	C'est une voiture *électronique*
Do you have an *electronic* train set?	As-tu un ensemble de trains *électroniques*

986. *expression/expression*

The *expression* on her face was worth it	*L'expression* sur son visage vaut le coup
He had a nice *expression* when hearing you	Il avait une bonne *expression* quand il t'écoutait
Look at her *expression* on seeing the gifts!	Regarde son *expression* quand elle voit les cadeaux

987. *feeling/sentiment*

I hold strange *feelings*	Je garde un *sentiment* étrange
I am having tender *feelings* now	J'ai des *sentiments* doux maintenant
I have confused *feelings*	j'ai des *sentiments* confus

988. *finish/finir*

Did you *finish* the job?	As-tu *fini* le travail?
When did you *finish* the work?	Quand as-tu *fini* le travail?
He will *finish* the job by tomorrow	Il va *finir* le travail demain

989. *fresh/frais*

I want some *fresh* eggs	Je veux quelques oeufs *frais*
Eat more *fresh* vegetables.	Manges plus de légumes *frais*
This food is not fresh	Ces aliments ne sont pas *frais*

990. *hear/entendre*

I *hear* music	*J'entends* la musique
Do you *hear* me?	Est-ce que tu *m'entends*?
I cannot *hear* it	Je ne peux pas *l'entendre*

991. *immediate/immédiat*

Tom's response was *immediate*	La réponse de Tom était *immédiate*
The medicine had an *immediate* effect	Le médicamment avait un effet

	immédiat
The effect was *immediate.*	L'effet était *immédiat*

992. *importance/importance*

This museum has lost its *importance*	Ce musée a perdu son *importance*
What is the *importance* of this dossier?	C'est quoi *l'mportance* de ce dossier
This matter is of prime *importance*	Cette affaire est de première *importance*

993. *normal/normal*

Everything looks *normal*	Tout semble *normal*
He thinks that is *normal.*	Il pense que c'est *normal*
It is healthy and *norma*l	C'est sain et *normal*

994. *opinion/opinion*

I have an *opinion*	J'ai une *opinion*
I agree with your *opinion*	Je suis d'accord avec ton *opinion*
His *opinion* was not accepted.	Son *opinion* n'était pas acceptée

995. *otherwise/autrement*

I heard *otherwise*	J'ai entendu *autrement*
I could not do *otherwise*	J'ai pas pu faire *autrement*

Do not ever think *otherwise*	Ne penses jamais *autrement*

996. *pair/paire*

He bought a *pair* of shoes	Il a acheté une *paire* de chaussures
Nancy wants a *pair* of red shoes	Nancy veut une *paire* de chaussures rouge
I have to buy a new *pair* of socks	Je dois acheter une nouvelle *paire* de chaussettes

997. *payment/paiement*

He demanded *payment* of the debt	Il a demandé un *paiement* de sa dette
Payment is required in advance	Le *paiement* est obligatoire à l'avance
They are pushing me for *payment*	Ils me poussent à *payer*

998. *plus/plus*

He has a huge bag *plus* a suitcase	Il a un énorme sac en *plus* de la valise
The *plus* sign should be on his car	Le signe *plus* doit etre sur sa voiture
All ambulances carry a *plus* sign.	Toutes les ambulances portent un signe *plus*

999. *press/presse-appuyer*

The *press* should be informed about this	La *presse* doit etre informée sur ça

Press the button to call the driver	*Appuie* sur le bouton pour appeler le chauffeur
You must *press* the alarm at once	Tu dois *appuyer* sur l'alarme en une fois

1000. *reality/réalité*

I like fiction rather than *reality*	J'aime la fiction plus que la *réalité*
The *reality* is not what it seems	La *réalité* n'est pas ce qu'il parait
Reality is different from fiction	La *réalité* est différente de la fiction

49417681R00156

Made in the USA
Middletown, DE
15 October 2017